THEODICY

THEODICY

Edited by
Dan Cohn-Sherbok

Jewish Studies
Volume 18

The Edwin Mellen Press
Lewiston/Queenston/Lampeter

Library of Congress Cataloging-in-Publication Data

Theodicy / edited by Dan Cohn-Sherbok.
    p.   cm. -- (Jewish studies ; v. 18)
    Includes bibliographical references.
    ISBN 0-7734-8690-9
    1. Suffering--Religious aspects--Judaism--History of Doctrines.
    2. Theodicy. I. Cohn-Sherbok, Dan. II. Series: Jewish studies
    (Lewiston, N.Y.) ; v. 18.
    BM645.S9T48 1997
    296.3'118--dc21   97-3725
                                                   CIP

This is volume 18 in the continuing series
Jewish Studies
Volume 18 ISBN 0-7734-8690-9
JS Series ISBN 0-88946-251-8

Studies in Jewish Theology Volume 4

A CIP catalog record for this book is available from the British Library.

The Edwin Mellen Press   The Edwin Mellen Press
Box 450   Box 67
Lewiston, New York   Queenston, Ontario
USA 14092-0450   CANADA L0S 1L0

The Edwin Mellen Press, Ltd.
Lampeter, Ceredigion, Wales
UNITED KINGDOM SA48 8LT

Printed in the United States of America

CONTENTS

PREFACE

Recently there has been a renewed interest in Jewish theology. Across the religious spectrum Jewish thinkers have been wrestling with fundamental questions about the nature of God and His activity. In part this interest has been generated by the religious perplexities resulting from the destruction of six million Jews during the Holocaust. In this question writers have looked to Biblical and rabbinic sources in an effort to formulate their own theological views.

The purpose of this series is to provide a forum for this theological reflection. These studies in Jewish theology will focus on a wide range of issues including: revelation, divine intervention and miracles, theodicy, the Hereafter, providence, the Messiah, and Jewish Christian relations. Most of the volumes will consist of essays by leading Jewish thinkers from all the branches of the Jewish faith. Other books in the series will be monographs by distinguished theologians on specific topics.

The first collection in this series, <u>Problems in Contemporary Jewish Theology</u>, concentrated on the nature of contemporary Jewish theology. Contributors included: Louis Jacobs, Jacob Neusner, Byron L. Serwin, David Blumenthal, Norbert M. Samuelson, Richard L. Rubenstein, Marc H. Elis, Raphael Loewe, David Novak, Hyam Maccoby, Norman Solomon, and Manfred H. Vogel.

The second volume, <u>Torah and Revelation</u>, continued this contemporary discussion about the central issues facing Jewish religious thought. Beginning with Arthur Green's Exploration of the character of Jewish theology, the book focused on such issues as propositional and non-propositional revelation, Scriptural interpretation, revelation as interpretation, the nature of Torah, Maimonides' conception of divine disclosure, Jewish-Christian dialogue and revelation, God and humanity, divine legislation, the concept of a Written Torah, and the progressive interpretation of revelation.

The third volume, <u>Divine Interventions and Miracles</u>, begins with an overview of the topic by Leo Trepp and Eliezer Schweid, and continues with a discussion of the liturgical dimensions of miraculous events, the philosophical concept of miracles, the interrelation between time and creation, divine intervention and religious sensibility, and miracles understood within a Hasidic framework.

This fourth volume, Theodicy, continues this exploration by focusing on the religious perplexities of divine justice. Beginning with an overview of theodicy by Norbert M Samuelson, the volume continues with a discussion of various philosophical aspects of this concept, theodicy and anti-theodicy in Jewish literature, the concept of suffering and Tish'ah B'av, the character of apophatic knowledge in Maimonidies' thought, and the challenges presented by the Holocaust to religious belief.

Those who have contributed to the volumes in the series have opened the debate. It is hoped that others will be stimulated by their observations, and, as readers, become participants in this open-ended exploration of the vital religious issues facing the Jewish people on the threshold of the twenty-first century.

Dan Cohn Sherbok

Chapter I

THEODICY

Norbert M. Samuelson

The so-called problem of theodicy[1] involves positing three propositions which appear to be mutually incoherent. They are: (A) God is perfectly good (B) God is perfectly powerful. And (C) there is evil. Any two of these three may be asserted without contradiction, but one of the three must be denied. God may be (B) perfectly powerful and (A) good if (~C) there is no evil. Conversely, there can be (C) evil if (~B) God has limited power and/or (~A) is not good. In general, the problem is resolved by denying any combination of the three propositions.[2] Of course which of these options is chosen depends on what theologians mean when they say "God", "good", "evil", "power", and how the adverb "perfectly" modifies these affirmations.

Throughout the course of the history of Jewish thought every possible move has been made to varying degrees, and several of them have been made in radically different ways. I will limit myself here to only three of what I consider to be the most interesting examples.

The View of the Torah - God is neither perfectly good nor powerful
The View of Genesis.

Whatever were the views of the different authors who wrote the different parts of the Pentateuch, a fairly consistent picture of the universe emerges from the text that the Jewish people inherited from its priestly editors in the sixth century

B.C.E.. That picture contains one fairly specific version of the problem of theodicy and poses a clear solution to it.[3] The problem focuses on a fairly specific event, viz. the destruction of the first Temple and the Exile of the people of Judea to Babylonia. According to this view God created the Universe for a single primary purpose - to provide the space and time for sacrifices to be offered to him. The successful fulfilment of these acts constitutes the end by which all actions are judged to be good or bad. In this context moral values are applied both ontically and socially. Ontically the term "good" is associated with separation and order. At first the universe exists as a single, homogeneous whole that is judged to be chaos. Gradually God introduces a set of distinctions, all of which are understood to overcome chaos and are called "good".[4] The progression of separations function at two levels simultaneously, one involving the space of the universe and the other involving the occupants of that space. Light is separated from dark, sky from earth, dry land from the seas on the surface of the earth, the land of Israel from other lands, and eventually [5] Mt. Zion, from other locals within the land of Israel, the space of the Temple from Mt. Zion, and the space of the Holy of Holies from the Temple mount. At the same time, the inhabitants of sphere of the earth are separated from the inhabitants of the sky, humanity from other living creatures on and in the sphere of the earth, the nations that descend from Abraham from the other nations that descend from Noah, Israel from the other families of Abraham, the Levites from other Israelites and eventually the Cohanim from the other Levites. The concluding ontic goods - a separate priest class who performs its defining function in a separate space - are themselves not mentioned in the Pentateuchal narrative. But their existence is always present throughout the narrative as the end towards which the biblical story points beyond itself. They are the paradigmatic references for the term "holy" (*Kadosh*), a term that functions within the narrative for what is of ultimate value. They are holy because they are separate, but they are separate because of the key role they play in making actual the purpose for which the universe was created - viz., the literal "service" [6] of God.

Socially the term "good" is associated with obeying God's Commandments. The differentiated regions of space are commanded to generate living occupants without limit, while the light inhabitants are ordered to rule their celestial region and the human inhabitants are commanded to govern their terrestrial region. The nations of humanity are given a set of laws beyond procreation to govern their society, while Israel, in the middle book of the five books,[7] is given an extensive law code to create a nation whose central purpose is to carry out the sacrificial laws described within the very heart of that middle book. Israel is constituted to be a nation whose primary task is to prepare meals where the holy people in their holy space dine with the holy God of the universe three times per day on weekdays and four times per day on the holy Sabbath. During the week there is labour as well as feast, but on the Sabbath there is only feast. More precisely, it is a day of continuous feast, for both God and humanity. It is this day that provides the Torah's primary vision of the end of days. Sabbath is the goal towards which all of creation points. It is the paradigm by which all good and evil are to be judged.

It is this cosmic scheme that is the context of the biblical version of the problem of theodicy. There exists evil, viz., the Temple has been destroyed, so that the priests cannot perform the tasks for which Israel exists, for which the universe was created. Evil exists because Israel failed to obey God's commandments. Hence, the God of the Pentateuch is not perfectly powerful, for there is service that he needs that he cannot perform himself. Clearly he is more powerful than anything else in the universe. He and he alone, after all, is the force that can either create or destroy it. But that power has limits. Similarly, but less obviously, he is not perfectly good. He performs acts of which he must repent, i.e., acts that fail to bring about his desired ends, not the least of which is the creation of humanity. Certainly from this respect - viz., the human - he is not perfect. For humanity exists within the universe for God; neither God nor the universe exists for the sake of humanity. Clearly he is better than anything else in the universe. He and he alone, after all, defines what is good and what is bad. But that goodness, like his power, has limits[8]

Classical Rabbinic philosophy - While God is perfectly good and powerful, there really is no evil - The Views of Maimonides and Gersonides

The solution to the pentateuchal problem of theodicy provided the framework for the development of the second Jewish polity under the policies of Ezra and Nehemiah. The new Judah became a state that remained faithful to its Toraitic constitution, viz., to serve God no matter what the human price. With the rise of Hellenism that price became enormous. Because Judah refused to reconstitute itself into an acceptable political model within the hellenistic world, it became the poorest of nations within the empire, and because it believed that its deity was the ultimate power in the universe, it fought three disastrous wars against the pagan Romans. Judah's failure to win those wars constituted a second, major occasion for the redefinition of theodicy within the perspective of Jewish thought. Scripture taught that the first Temple had been destroyed because Israel had failed to keep God's commandments. But the second Temple was destroyed precisely because the nation did obey God's law. Clearly, if God is the creator of the physical world, the universe should now come to an end, and, it if does not, then its continued survival must be for some other reasons than continual communal dining by a small portion of humanity with the creator God of the universe. In other words, it cannot be true that the destruction of the second Temple is really evil. Rather, it must serve as some yet unrecognised divine good. Furthermore, if even the destruction of the Temple is not really evil, then all the lesser evils from a human perspective must not really be evil. But what could that purpose be and why does it remain hidden from even the chosen people of God's humanity?

The second Moses - viz., Moses Maimonides - provides a second myth in his *Guide of the Perplexed* [9] to solve the second paradigm fact of evil. Again, the first paradigm was the destruction of the first Temple, whose cosmic solution was presented in the name of the first Moses as the myth of creation. The second paradigm is the destruction of the second Temple, whose cosmic solution is hinted at by Moses Maimonides in his myth of the Sabians.[10]

Maimonides reports the following story. The universe as God created it was perfect, as was everything within it. More precisely, everything was created to be perfectly what it was supposed to be. That does not mean that anything created was absolutely perfect. If everything were absolutely perfect, then everything would have been God, and there would not have been a world other than God.[11] Rather, the universe as a whole was perfectly a universe, and everything within it was perfectly what it had been created to be, including Adam, the first man. That Adam was perfectly a man entails that he was no less, but also no more, than a human male. With respect to knowledge, he knew perfectly everything that a human could know, but he knew nothing that was beyond human knowledge. In general that meant that he understood everything that he perceived through his senses and he had the mental ability to make valid logical inferences from that experience, but he had no views on any subject the knowledge of which was beyond the limits of experience. The topics of such trans-empirical based knowledge fall under the general heading of metaphysics. It includes cosmology, cosmogony and theology. Angels are capable of such knowledge, but not human beings. At best people can have opinions, but they have no basis to know whether or not those opinions are in fact true. And Adam, being a perfect human, knew only what he knew he could know, viz., physics, and did not even think about what he could not know, viz., metaphysics.

However, humanity also had the ability to extend its powers beyond the original nature. Its first extension was to develop agriculture. By nature what grows are a mixture of plants, some of which are fit for human consumption and others of which are not. By the simplest act of farming, viz., weeding out what they could not eat, to leave more room for what he could, the first humans made nature (from a human perspective) better, and by so doing made it unnatural. From this beginning developed a nation of farmers, known as the Sabians [12] who extended all of their abilities beyond the confines of the human species into the power domain of the angels. However, in so improving themselves, they introduced into the world error and sin. In other words, by improving the universe for humanity they in fact made it less perfect in itself than it had been. The problem was that while the original human was perfectly human, the improved human was imperfectly angelic. While humans limited their thought to what humans could know, they reasoned without error, but when they improved themselves to reason about what only the angels and God could know, they reasoned badly, i.e., they made mistakes that had dire consequences for both humanity and the universe.

The Sabians drew an analogy between their farms and the universe. Their land lacked human order and value until they, the farmers, imposed structure upon it, transforming it from a wasteland into farms. Similarly, the universe as a whole exhibits order and value. Hence, by analogy, just as they had imposed structure on one segment of the space of the universe, so there must be an entity, who, like a farmer, imposed divine order and value on what had originally been the disordered, valueless space of the universe. That entity is the Creator of the Universe, the only being worthy of worship as a deity. But who would that God be? The question was right. The order of the universe does suggest that it exists by intention and not by accident, and the existence of an intelligent product does suggest an intelligent producer. But, again, this is a question for divine entities to ponder, not for mere humans, who, in consequence of their limitations, gave false answers. They looked about them for what they could find to be the most excellent entities within the realm of their experience to worship as deity. Rightly their attention focused on the celestial beings - the sun, the moon, and the constellations, who they proclaimed to be their gods. Their reasoning was correct as far as it could go. What is most excellent is most worthy of worship, and of all that they could experience the living entities of the sky are most excellent. But they are not the creator; they are merely creatures. The true creator lay beyond anything that could be given within the domain of human experience. Hence, the first humans progressed from having no religion, like animals, to worshipping deity, like angels. But the religion they formed was profane. Having transcended the appropriate agnosticism of their origin where they knew nothing about deities, they became idolaters, who worshipped false gods, the gravest form of sin, for the universe had been created to serve its creator, not creatures.

The human decline from human perfection in its advance beyond primordial human nature had equally dire consequences in ethics. Originally human beings did not think about what is right and what is wrong. They behaved naturally without reflection. However, as they developed their ability to manipulate nature, they came to realise that humans need not always act in accord with their nature, that in fact they could deliberate and make choices that were counter-intuitive. They then began to think about what they ought and ought not to do, and in so doing, because of their limitations as human beings, they made bad decisions, often disastrous, decisions that eventually led to the corruption of the generation of Noah, corruption so profound that it threatened the survival of the universe as a whole. In consequence, God was forced to destroy humanity through a universal flood and to begin his universe anew. But this second beginning differed from the first. Recognising that humanity could not remain forever within the confines of human nature, God provided a political model for humanity to develop a kind of society in which it could know the difference between metaphysical truth and error as well as moral right and wrong. That model is the Torah that God revealed to Moses at Sinai.

Torah is here understood to be a national constitution that has universal consequences. Through obedience to its law, Israel could in time develop into a kingdom of angels, who, armed with celestial wisdom, could lead the rest of humanity to an end of days when all human beings would become divine.

So much for what Maimonides explicitly states in the text of the Guide. Of course the problem is that Israel, being very human, cannot understand adequately what the Torah says, including the reasons for its social legislation. Hence, Israel, like all of humanity, always has the option, through ignorance, to choose to disobey. To the extent that Israel disobeys, it prevents the coming the end of days; to the extent that Israel obeys, it hastens that coming. Maimonides believed that progress toward the messianic ideal of an end of days was more likely than decline towards the Noaitic flood limit of an end to the universe, and that the destruction of the second Jewish commonwealth itself contributed to that positive evolution. Furthermore, he believed that to whatever extent Israel obeyed God's law, it improved its moral and conceptual talents, and to the extent that Israel so improved, the possibility of even greater obedience to Toraitic law improved. Increasingly Israel, and eventually the rest of humanity, would understand God's purpose in creation, and through that understanding the apparent evils that occur in the world would become intelligible and, in consequence, avoidable. But progress would be slow, slower than even Maimonides himself anticipated.

It is against the background of the myth of the Sabians that we should understand what explicitly Maimonides says about theodicy. From an absolute perspective, God is perfectly good and powerful and there really is no evil. To be sure from this perspective the created universe is not perfect. But it could not be and still be the world. It is, as Leibniz would later say, the best of all possible worlds. In other words, while the universe is not perfect, because it cannot be better than it is, its imperfection does not constitute real evil. In fact, the only evil is human ignorance, a defect that the Torah was created to overcome.

How ignorant are we? *Prima facie* Maimonides suggests that it is absolute. The distance between what we know of God and the universe as it is in itself is infinite, and, because it is infinite, it is unbridgeable. But this surface reading of Maimonides' words cannot be correct, for it if were, then, no matter how our wisdo improves, we would be no closer to the messianic ideal, and, if there can be n progress, then the legislation of the Torah would have no practical value. On hand, it is clear that for Maimonides the actual world is infinitely remote from the divine ideal, but, on the other hand, it must be possible to progress towards it. The reconciliation of these apparent opposites is found in Maimonides' negative theology.[13]

The critical datum underlying Maimonides', and all subsequent Jewish philosophic, analysis of God-talk is that God and God alone is the creator while everything else is a creature. Hence, there is a fundamental difference between God and everything else, a difference so extreme that no positive human language can literally be applied to God. A general term can be predicated of any number of subjects in the same way (i.e., with the same meaning) only if in the relevant respects these subjects belong to the same species. Where a single general term is predicated of two or more subjects from different species, the meaning of the subsequent sentences is radically different. (E.g., "The boy is big" and "Government is big"). In such cases, the meaning of the stated general term is equivocal. In what way equivocal and how the different uses are related depends on the way the relevant subject species differ. Whatever these ways are, it is most extreme in the case where a single term is predicated of both God and anything else, for here there cannot even be a common genus, let alone a common species.

In subsequent centuries Maimonides was understood to have been defending the claim that the difference is so radical that any attribution of anything to God is, from a human perspective, unintelligible. As an alternative, Gersonides offered a less extreme, theologically more acceptable account of the difference in meaning between predication of God and anything else.[14] Basing himself on the way that Aristotle in his *Metaphysics* applied the term "*ousia*" to a substance and any other kind of subject, Gersonides judged divine attributes to be *pros hen* equivocal, i.e., to apply primarily to God and secondarily to anything else so that the secondary usages are dependent on the primary usage in the following two ways: (a) The meaning of the predicate term when applied to something other than God contains a reference to its primary divine meaning, so that the truth of the secondary meaning is logically entailed by the truth of the primary meaning, and (b) the fact described in the sentence that contains the secondary predication is causally dependent on the state described in the sentence that contains the primary predication. For example, to say that certain persons are good states something about how those people are related to God, viz., that what it means to say that they are good involves a statement about how they are related to God's goodness, and that God is the ultimate cause of their goodness. In brief, statements about the Creator express ideals which, as such, are related to comparable statements about all and any creatures of God.

How the two classic Jewish interpretations of divine attributes, viz. those of Maimonides and Gersonides, are different is not obvious.[15] On final analysis Maimonides may have intended something like what Gersonides subsequently spelled out. In fact, given the way that Maimonides' theory of divine attributes was interpreted by Hermann Cohen's disciples, there is little difference.[16] For both Jewish philosophers divine attributes express ideals that are related, as a primary and a final cause, to what is actual. All divine attributes express God.[17] But the actual in principle never is God.[18] The term "Creator" expresses God's relationship to the world as its first cause. He is the source from which the universe unfolds. And the term "Redeemer" expresses God's relationship to the world as its final cause. He is the telos towards which it moves. The perceived universe of time and space persists between these two transcendent poles of origin and end.

Modern Jewish philosophy - While God is perfectly good, he is not perfectly powerful - The Views of Hermann Cohen, Martin Buber & Franz Rosenzweig.

On Cohen's understanding of Maimonides (and through Maimonides, of authentic Judaism), divine attributes are to be understood as moral ideals.[19] In general, given any simple, affirmative predicate, P, what it means to say that God is P is that God is not Q, where Q is the complement of P. Hence, to say that God is good means that He is not bad, that He is powerful means that He is not weak, etc. The problem is, however, that to be able to predicate any P of God would render God-talk unintelligible, but why can we not say God is Q, which correctly means that literally God is not P, since no attribute literally understood can be predicated of God? Maimonides' answer is that we may predicate of God only those attributes that the Torah affirms of Him, and the reason why Scripture says what it says is because the affirmed attributes are all human excellences. In other words, all statements about God are in reality disguised moral imperatives, where a statement of the narrative form, "God is P" means the commandment, "Strive to become P". What links the declaration to the imperative is the principle of holiness, viz., "You shall be holy as I the Lord your God am holy" (Lev 19.2). In other words, the content of theological statements about God are entirely ethical, and the religion of the people of Israel who proclaim them is a political program to redeem the world. This Cohenian reading of Maimonides' theology has informed all subsequent Jewish theology.

From this perspective, the problem of theodicy dissolves.[20] As a moral ideal God is perfectly good. More accurately He is "the" good. But as moral ideal God is perfectly good. More accurately He is "the" good. But as an ideal He has power only to guide. The actual work of the transformation of the universe into something good is the obligation of human beings. They and they alone, in all of their imperfection, have the power to realise moral values in lived life. The nature of the world as God created it has order and structure, but that order is morally neutral. On this understanding of the biblically based faith of Israel, what Genesis means when it says that God called His creation "good" is that He has produced one kind of creature, the human, whose task is to create good, i.e., to transform what are ontically only things into something socially of value. In other word, God creates the human, but it is the human who creates value.

Cohenian Judaism posits two ways to view reality - narratively as it is viewed in natural science and history as something that is, and imperatively as it is viewed in religion and ethics as something that is not what it ought to be. The former way views the world in terms of objects subject to physical laws. The latter way views it in terms of personal relationships subject to moral rules. From the former perspective, there is no evil. There are only facts and fictions that are either intelligible or unintelligible. From the latter perspective there are only occasions that create moral obligations which may or may not be obeyed. Buber called the former the I-It relationship and the latter the I-Thou. Within his language God is "I-Eternal Thou", by which he meant that God functions perfectly as the paradigm for human moral obligation. Rosenzweig formed a picture of the reality where life is lived between these two perspectives. The former is the fore-world (*Vorwelt*) of things that he calls "elements". The latter is the over-world (*Uberwelt*) of ideals that he calls "structure" (Gestalt). Lived life in the world is an infinite set of movements from distinct nothings of things toward individual somethings of value. Infinitely remote at both ends of the flow of human and physical history is God, as an element at the creation of the world, and as truth at its redemption. As such, God is not of the world, even though He is what makes it intelligible. He is never actual, but He is ultimately, ideally, all that really-truly is. There is a deep divide between what is actual and what is true that human beings in the world bridge through God.

To be sure there are important differences between the Jewish philosophies of Cohen, Buber and Rosenzweig. But they do not differ in the general guidelines that they inherited from Maimonides' expression of biblical theology. Consequently, they share in common, albeit in different languages, the same reconciliation of the problem of theodicy. Only God is good, only what exists in the world has power, and only humanity has the power to make good a world that inherently is not.

Concluding Remarks

Our story of the history of what Jewish philosophy has to say about theodicy is now concluded. It is worth noting that the two main classical Jewish accounts of theodicy arose in response to specific events, viz., the destruction of the first Temple for the editors of the Torah and the destruction of the second Temple for the rabbinic philosophers. In contrast the modern Jewish philosophers presupposed no such paradigmatic event for their speculation. If there is one, it would have happened after they wrote their major works. It would have been the Holocaust. Several contemporary Jewish theologians believe that this event requires a rethinking of Jewish theology no less radical than the changes required by the destruction of the second Temple. The most notable of these thinkers is Emil Fackenheim.[21] He argues that the Holocaust is so demonic and so distinct that it nullifies the truth value of all previous philosophy, including Jewish philosophy, and it renders all subsequent philosophy, including Jewish philosophy, impossible. Personally I do not share this radical judgement. While the Holocaust was a great disaster for both the Jewish people and for the world, it does not merit a conceptual status that is qualitatively beyond that of the destruction of the first two Temples. Nor does it raise anything conceptually new beyond what the above accounts of theodicy, all other factors being equal, can handle. None of this is intended to minimalise either the great evil of the Holocaust or its critical importance for contemporary Jewish history and life. It is only to say that in itself the Holocaust raises no special perspective for solving, or at least attempting to solve, the problem of theodicy.

In conclusion, there are a number of features of the above description of Jewish philosophic accounts of theodicy that I would like to highlight. First, the problem of evil is seen in terms of collectives rather than individuals. For Rosenzweig, as for the editors of the Torah, moral issues range primarily over nations and only secondarily over their citizens. In general, in marked contrast to most modern thought, individuals exist as parts of collective; collectives are not mere mental groupings of individuals. Second, judgements of individual events as good or bad are based on teleology. No event in itself has moral value. The universe is either viewed ontologically from a scientific perspective, in which case moral judgements are inappropriate, or from a political perspective, in which case events are judged from the perspective of a revealed vision of both the origin (creation) and the end (redemption) of the universe. Third, neither standard of judgement, creation or redemption, are, ever were, or ever will be anything actual in the perceptible world of time and space. Rather, they are always ideals that function perpetually for humanity to know that what is is not good and can always become better. It is in this sense that all of the solutions to the problem of theodicy turn on positing myths. Here the term "myth" functions in much the same way that Plato used it in the *Timaeus*,[22] viz., as a picture or story or model that is inherently something more than opinion but less than knowledge, that as such is somewhat, but not entirely, intelligible.

NOTES

1. The following essay is a development beyond an earlier piece I wrote on theodicy from a Jewish perspective entitled "Solutions of Theodicy out of the Sources of Judaism", *Religious Education 84*,1 (Winter, 1989) 55-67.

2. viz. (1) ~ABC, (2) ~A~BC, (3) AB~C, (4) A~BC, (5) ~AB~C, (6) ~A~B~C, and (7) A~B~C.

14

3. What follows in this section are conclusions based on what I believe to be a reasonably rigorous literary analysis of the Hebrew text, particularly the first chapter of Genesis, in my *The First Seven Days: A Philosophical Commentary on the Creation of Genesis* Atlanta, GA: Scholars Press, 1993. Other books particularly relevant to this interpretation are the following: Robert Alter, *The Art of Biblical Narrative*, New York, Basic Books, 1981. Umberto Cassuto, *A Commentary on the Book of Genesis*, translated into English by Israel Abrahams; Jerusalem, Magnes, 1961-1964. Michael Fishbane, *Text and Texture: Close Readings of Selected Biblical Texts*, New York, Schocken, 1979. Yehezkiel Kaufmann, *The Religion of Israel: From Its Beginnings to the Babylonian Exile*, translated into English by Moshe Greenberg, Chicago, University of Chicago Press, 1960. Jon D.Levenson, *Creation and the Persistence of Evil: The Jewish Drama of Divine Omnipotence*, San Francisco, Harper and Row, 1988. Jon D.Levenson, *Sinai and Zion: An Entry into the Jewish Bible*, San Francisco, Harper and Row, 1987. Nahum M. Sarna, *The JPS Torah Commentary Genesis*, translation and commentary by Nahum M. Sarna, Philadelphia, Jewish Publication Society, 1989.

4. The terms explicitly employed in the biblical narrative are "good" (tov) and "chaos" (tohu vavohu), which are understood to be opposites, which entails that "order" (*seder*) is associated with good while "evil" (*ra*) is associated with chaos, even though these latter terms are not explicitly used in this way in the biblical text. However, the association of these sets of terms will be made explicit in subsequent (medieval) rabbinic, philosophic commentaries on the biblical text.

5. I.e., beyond the time line of the Pentateuchal narrative, which concludes as Israel begins to take possession of its land and create a nation, a nation whose destruction concludes the narratives of the Hebrew Scriptures. It is this concluding event that is the problem that biblical theodicy addresses.

6. The Hebrew term is "*avodah*", whose concrete referent is the sacrificial activity of the Temple cult. It is the detailed description of this literal divine service that occupies the central (and therefore most important) place within this literary composition by the exiled Babylonian priests who edited the Torah.

7. Viz., in Leviticus. On the Judgement that the editors of the Pentateuch followed a onion-like, as opposed to a linear, structure in constructing the Torah, so that what is most important is set in the middle of otherwise parallel texts in the extreme, see Jacob Milgrom's commentary on the Book of Numbers, *The JPS Torah Commentary: Numbers*, Philadelphia/New York, The Jewish Publication Society, 1990, especially pp.xvi-xxixx of the Introduction.

8. How close Maimonides believed himself and his generation to be to the messianic age is a subject of scholarly debate. There have been several articles on this question in recent years, but none of them are decisive. Here and in what follows I accept the view of Steven Schwarzschild that the Messianic Age functioned for Maimonides as an asymptote, i.e., as an ideal limit intended to provide humanity with a model for moral judgements that can in actuality be approached but never realised. Cf. Schwarzschild, Steven S. "Moral Radicalism and 'Middlingness' in the Ethics of Maimonides" *Studies in Medieval Culture* 11 (1977) 65-94, reprinted in Menachem Kellner, ed., *The Pursuit of the Ideal: Jewish Writings of Steven Schwarzschild*, Albany State University of New York Press, 1990, pp.137-160.

9. Moses Ibn Maimon (Maimonides). *Dalalah Alcha-Idin (The Guide of the Perplexed)* [*moreh nevukhim*]. Translated into Hebrew by Judah Ibn Tibbon. Wilna, I.Funk, 1904. Translated into Hebrew by Joseph Bahir David Kapach, Jerusalem, *Musad Ha-Rav Kook*, 1972. Translated into French by Solomon Munk, Paris, A.Franck, 1856-1866. Translated into English by Shlomo Pines, Chicago, University of Chicago Press, 1963. Henceforth referred to as "Guide".

10. In the Guide Book III, chapter 29.

11. This explanation of why everything was not absolutely perfect is not explicitly stated by Maimonidies in the passage in question. However, it is implied. My explicit statement is a summary of what Maimonides' predecessor, Abraham Ibn Daud, said in his *The Exalted Faith*, Book 2, Basic Principle

6, chapter 2, 203b 16-204b16 of the Mich 57 manuscript in Oxford University's Bodleian Library of Solomon Ibn Labi's Hebrew translation from the original Judeo-Arabic. Cf. Abraham Ben David Ha-Levi (Ibn Daud), *The Exalted Faith (Ha-Emunah Ha-Ramah)* edited by Norbert M Samuelson and Gershon Weiss; translated into English by Norbert M. Samuelson, Cranbury, N.J., Associated University Presses, 1986; pp.242, 246-247,251.

12.Who the Sabians of Maimonides' myth/story might be is a topic of scholarly debate. My personal guess is that they are the Chaldeans.

13.The secondary literature on Maimonides' theory of divine attributes is vast. While it is never perfectly clear what Maimonides in fact believed he was saying about any topic that is critical to his philosophy, some positions seems more coherent with the totality of his writings than others. In this article I accept the general guidelines of Hermann Cohen and his disciples who understand Maimonides' negative theology to mean that divine attributes state moral, asymptotic ideas. Even confined to the Cohenian interpretation of divine attributes, the relevant bibliography would be too large to present in this article. Instead, I will limit my references to Zevi Diesendruck, "The Philosophy of Maimonides". *Central Conference of American Rabbis Yearbook LXV* (1935): pp.355-368, and the following three articles by me (the last of which bearing most directly on the interpretation presented here): "On Knowing God: Maimonides, Gersonides and the Philosophy of Religion", *Judaism* (Winter,1969) pp.64-77. "The Role of Politics in the Torah According to Maimonides, Spinoza and Buber," *Community and Culture: Essays in Jewish Studies,* edited by Nahum M.Waldman, Philadelphia, Gratz College Seth Press, 1987, pp.193-208. "Divine Attributes as Moral Ideals in Maimonides' Theology," *The Thought of Maimonides: Philosophical and Legal Studies,* edited by Ira Robinson, Lawrence Kaplan and Julien Bauer, *Studies in the History of Philosophy,* Volume 17, Lewiston/Queenston/Lampeter, Edwin Mellon Press, 1991, pp.69-76.

14.In Levi Ben Gershon (Gersonides), *Milchamot Adonai (The Wars of the Lord)* III-IV, Riva di Trento, s.n., 1560 and Leipzig, K.B.Lark, 1866, translated into German by B.Kellerman, *Die Kampfe Gott's von Lewi Ben Gerson,* Berlin, Mayer and Muller, 1914. Book III is translated into English by Norbert M.Samuelson, *Gersonides on God's Knowledge,* Toronto, Pontifical Institute of Medieval Studies, 1977. Book IV is translated into English by J.David Bleich, *Providence in the Philosophy of Gersonides,* New York, Yeshiva University Press, 1973. Books III and IV are translated into French by Charles Touati, *Les Guerres du Seigneur, Livres 3 et 4,* Paris, Mouton, 1968. Also see Charles Touati, *La pensee Philosophique et Theologique de Gersonides,* Paris, Minuit, 1973, and the following works by me: "On Knowing God: Maimonides, Gersonides and the Philosophy of Religion,"*Judaism* (Winter, 1969) pp.64-77. "Gersonides' Account of God's Knowledge of Particulars," *Journal of the History of Philosophy* (October, 1972) pp.399-416. "The Tenth Principle- Omniscience- Gersonides, *Milhamot Ha-Shem,* Third Treatise, chapters 1,3-6," *With Perfect Faith: The Foundations of Jewish Belief,* J.David Bleich (ed.)., New York, Ktav, 1983, pp.440-466.

15. This is a topic that should be, but has not as yet been, adequately discussed by contemporary students of medieval Jewish philosophy.

16. One other Jewish philosopher worthy of mention in this context with Maimonides and Gersonides is Baruch Spinoza. He has been omitted here from consideration only because of space limitations in this volume and because his influence on subsequent Jewish thought was mostly negative. Like his intellectual Jewish teachers, Maimonides and Gersonides, Spinoza affirms a God who is perfectly good and powerful and denies the reality of evil. However, his interpretation of these three claims stands in intentional and explicit opposition to their religious Jewish solutions of the problem of theodicy. What he objects to is their judgement that the world is good. Rather, Spinoza constructs a model for understanding where reality is morally neutral. The issue is not theodicy. It is science. And the source of the disagreement is how Spinoza interpreted what it meant for the Creator of the Universe to be perfect. The tradition of classical Jewish philosophy had argued that the universe and everything in it are perfectly what they are, which entails that they are not absolutely perfect. Spinoza understood this

judgement to mean that everything is the way it is because it must be that way. An absolutely perfect God must always do what is absolutely perfect, and since there is nothing else that can influence or modify what an absolutely perfect agent does, this universe is a necessary one, i.e., the only one that is logically and causally possible. Hence, there are no genuine options in the universe and without options it makes no sense to say that what happens in the universe happens for a purpose. God does what He does not to bring something about; God does what He does simply because He is God. This position also is a solution to the problem of theodicy. Like Maimonides Spinoza claims that what appears to be evil only appears so because of the inadequacy of human knowledge. However, Spinoza's solution - viz., to posit a non-moral universe - stands outside the dominant tradition of Jewish religious thought, which, as we shall see, makes ethics primary over ontology. Spinoza had enormous influence on the subsequent, so-called "modern" attitudes of educated Western civilisation. In this and many other respects Spinoza's philosophy was paradigmatic for the subsequent development of modern science, particularly in the humanities. However, his influence in Jewish thought was, rightly or wrongly, primarily negative. Spinoza's ontologically primary, morally neutral, algebraic picture of the universe stands in marked contrast to the ethically primary, calculus-process picture of the universe that Cohen and his disciples in modern Jewish philosophy developed.

17. For both Maimonides and Gersonides this is a consequence of God's radical unity. No attribute can express part of God, because God can have no parts. Similarly, no attribute can express something that merely is true of God, because then God could be other than He is, which, if that were possible, would entail that God could be influenced by something other than His own nature, which would entail that God is not perfectly powerful. Consequently, every divine attribute is God.

18. Cohen will say that to affirm anything actual as good would constitute idolatry, which is a consequence of both the radical separation between God as Creator and the world as His creation, and the radical separation in principle between the is and the ought.

19.The following works by Cohen are relevant to this discussion: *Des Prinzip der infinitesimal-Method,* Frankfurt a.M., Suhrkamp, 1968. *Jüdische Schriften,* edited by Franz Rosenzweig, Berlin, 1924, and *Religion der Vernunft aus den Quellen der Judentums,* Frankfurt a.M., 1929, translated into English by Simon Kaplan, *Religion of Reason,* New York, Ungar, 1972. Also relevant are the following secondary works: J.Klatzkin, *Hermann Cohen,* Berlin, 1921. William Kluback, *Hermann Cohen: The Challenge of a Religion of Reason,* Chico, Scholars Press, 1984, and J.Melber, *Hermann Cohen's Philosophy of Judaism,* New York, Jonathan David, 1968.

20.The following application of the philosophies of Martin Buber and Franz Rosenzweig to theodicy are based on my discussion of these three philosophers in chapters 10-11 of my *An Introduction to Modern Jewish Philosophy,* Albany, State University of New York Press, 1989. The "Recommended Readings" listed at the end of each chapter are the works upon which my interpretation is based. My reading of Buber is based primarily on his *Ich und Du* (Heidelberg, Verlag Lambert Schneider, 1977, translated into English by Walter Kaufmann, *I and Thou,* New York, Charles Scribner's Sons, 1970), as my reading of Rosenzweig is based primarily on his *Der Stern der Erlosung* (Rosenzweig, Franz, *Der Stern der Erlosung,* Frankfurt a.M., J.Kaufmann, 1921, translated into English by William W.Hallo, *The Star of Redemption,* Boston, Beacon Press, 1971, translated into Hebrew by Yehoshua Amir, *kokhav ha-geulah,* Jerusalem, Bialik Institute, 1970). The interested reader can find a more detailed expression of my understanding of these works in the following essays: "Rosenzweig's Concept of (Jewish) Ethics", *Joodse Filosofie Tussen Rede En Traditie: Feestbundelter ere van de tachtigste verjaardag van Prof.dr H.J.Herring,* edited by Reinier Munk, Amsterdam, Kok Kampen, 1993, pp.207-220. "The Concept of 'Nichts' in Rosenzweig's 'Star of Redemption'," *Der Philosoph Franz Rosenzweig (1886-1929),* Band II, Das neue Denken und seine Dimensionen, edited by Wolfdietrich Schmied-Kowarzik, Freiburg, Verlag Karl Alber, 1988, pp.643-656. "The Role of Politics in the Torah According to Maimonides, Spinoza and Buber,"*Community and Culture:Essays in Jewish Studies,* edited by Nahum M.Waldman, Philadelphia, Gratz College Seth Press, 1987, pp.193-208. "Halevi and Rosenzweig on Miracles", *Approaches to Judaism in Medieval Times,* edited by David R.Blumenthal, Brown Judaic Studies #54,

Chico, CA, Scholars Press, 1984, pp.157-172. "Ibn Daud and Franz Rosenzweig on Other Religions: A Contrast Between Medieval and Modern Jewish Philosophy," *Proceedings of the Eighth World Congress of Jewish Studies, Division C: Talmud and Midrash, Philosophy and Mysticism, Hebrew and Yiddish Literature,* Jerusalem, 1982, pp.75-80.

21.One should read all of his writings to see the development of his most original and insightful analysis. However, clearly his most mature, and conclusive, work is *To Mend the World: Foundations of Future Jewish Thought,* New York, Schocken, 1982.

22. 52b. There Plato invokes mythology, which he calls "bastard reasoning" (logismu tini nothu), as the appropriate way to talk about space (chora). See Richard Dakre Archer-Hind, *The Timaeus of Plato,* New York, Arno Press, 1973, and Francis MacDonald Cornford, *Plato's Cosmology,* London, Routledge & Kegan Paul, 1966 (first published by Kegan Paul, Trench, Trubner & Co., 1937).

Chapter II

THEODICY - SOME PHILOSOPHICAL ASPECTS
Ze'ev Levy

Leibniz's Theodicy and the responses of Kant and Hume

The concept (or term) of *theodicy* is composed of two Greek words - *theos* (God) and *dike* (justice). It means to elevate the sovereignty of God's will beyond all human measures of moral evaluation. The creator of the world and its supreme ruler is also the unquestioned authority on good and evil. This conception revokes the idea of moral reason that judges God's acts by the same criteria as human acts. The essence of theodicy is therefore the relation between God's justice, man's freedom and the existence of evil. Theodicy is evidently of relevance only for theistic theologies that conceive of the Deity as a personal God. The word was created and introduced into philosophical language, as well known, by G.W. Leibniz in his *Theodicee sur la bonte de Dieu, la liberte de l'homme et l'origine due mal* of 1710 (one of the few books published during his lifetime).

The problem itself was not a new one. It was discussed already in the Bible (Cain, the Binding of Isaac, and especially "Job"), became a subject of controversy among the Sages, reappeared in Christian and Islamic theology, was refuted by Maimonides,[1] and debated in Jewish medieval philosophy. It was usually formulated as *predestination*. Unlike determinism, the philosophical inference of causality, predestination is the belief that everything happens according to God's autonomous will.

In this matter I limit myself to the issue of theodicy in modern philosophy and Jewish thought, that is after Leibniz. Although I do not profess any religious outlook, it seems fascinating to me, how various modern thinkers tried to come to grips with this theological issue.

Leibniz wanted to vindicate the assertion that God's acts are intrinsically just and right. The evil that one encounters in the world is of human origin, but without the inevitable deficiencies in the world one would not be able to appreciate the good and the beautiful that prevail. This was derived from his famous assertion in the *Theodicee* that ours is "the best of all possible worlds". It was derived in its turn from his logical principle of sufficient reason. If ours is the best possible world, why is there evil? He treated this as a question of juridical responsibility, in order to refute Pierre Bayle's view that opposed reason to belief while according to him they can be reconciled harmoniously. The philosopher Fritz Mauthner (a Jew, estranged to Judaism) defined Leibniz's optimism as an "honorary salvation" ("*Ehrenrettung*") of God; it is the crux of his theodicy.[2]

Leibniz had coined the concept in order to justify God's goodness against the claims of the apparent existence of evil in the world; he tried to refute the latter on account of their allegedly atheistic consequences. He did not deny the existence of evil, but asserted that any other possible world would contain more evil than ours. Similar ideas were expressed also by his contemporaries A. Shaftesbury and A. Pope ("whatever is, is Right." "All partial evil, universal good.") Leibniz's closest pupil and collaborator, Christian Wolff, identified the term with philosophical theology in general, but all later philosophers and theologians employed it in its Leibnizian original sense. Also the North-Italian Jewish Rabbi and scholar S.D.Luzzatto still clung to the traditional version of theodicy.

> When there occurs an earthquake, and houses tumble down on their dwellers, or when pestilence rages in the land, and half of its inhabitants are wiped out, is it not God who ordered this?[3]

He probably had in mind the famous earthquake in Lisbon that caused various thinker of the Enlightenment, among others Goethe, to abandon their belief in God. Leibniz's argument aroused much critical response from their part although many of them were much impressed by Leibniz's philosophy in general. The most famous attack was, of course, Voltaire's *Candide ou sur l'optimisme* of 1759, while the most systematical refutation was Kant's *On the Failure of all philosophical attempts of theodicy* of 1791.[4]

Since theodicy is a human theological argument, it cannot base itself on the assumption of God's supreme wisdom; that would, according to Kant, presuppose the conclusions to be demonstrated. The advocates of theodicy must therefore resort to arguments of (human) reason in order to refute the claims raised against God's benevolence, omnipotence and purposeful providence. These three divine attributes are compromised morally by the existence of evil and sin, physically by the existence of pain and suffering, and juridically by the disproportion between sin and punishment. These put into question, each in its turn, God's capacity as a creator, his goodness and his justice.[5] The defenders of theodicy riposted by three counter arguments: 1. With regard to creation, human reason is inadequate to comprehend God's supreme wisdom. This is obviously no more than an apologetic evasion of the issue that needs no refutation. Or, evil is a result of man's finite nature, but then it cannot be qualified as a moral evil. 2. With regard to God's goodness, men prefer a life, even with pain and suffering, to the alternative of death. This is, according to Kant, mere sophistry, as is also the supplementary argument that pain in this world is a precondition for eternal bliss in the afterworld. 3. With regard to God's justice, the sinner, going unpunished in this world, suffers, as it were, from pangs of conscience. But Kant rightly comments that this is no more than ascribing to the sinner character-traits of a virtuous person which he precisely lacks. He also rejects as arbitrary the assumption that true reward and punishment will be everyone's lot only in the next world.[6] It follows from all this that the defenders of theodicy are unable to accomplish what they promised to prove. Kant tries to corroborate his outlook by the story of *Job*. Job does not justify God morally but merely acknowledges his own ignorance. (I shall still come back to *Job*.) But what is of the essence to Kant: morality must not be based on faith, but faith on morality.[7] He concludes his refutation of theodicy by relinquishing it to belief; it has no place in rational discourse or scientific inquiry.

Still before Kant, David Hume took up the gauntlet and returned to the age-old problem, already raised by Epicurus:

> Is he (God) willing to prevent evil, but unable? then he is impotent. Is he able, but not willing? then he is malevolent. is he both able and willing? Whence then is evil?[8]

Hume, the sceptic, left these questions unanswered, thus continuing, though inadvertently, an argumentation that was characteristic of many Jewish medieval philosophers, Kant, the agnostic, did not hesitate to give a definite answer and rejected theodicy unequivocally. [9]

Theodicy is mainly concerned with justifying God in spite of existing states of affairs that are incompatible with the assumption of his goodness. But what with God's express commands to perform acts that are unacceptable by our ethical standards, e.g. ordering Abraham to sacrifice Isaac, or his command to exterminate the peoples of Kana'an, including women and children, etc.? The most renowned attempt to overcome this ethical quandary was S.Kierkegaard's "*teleological suspension of ethics*" in *Fear and Trembling.* [10] This issue presents a serious challenge to theodicy, but transgresses the scope of the present inquiry.

Hermann Cohen's and Leo Baeck's positive approach to theodicy.

While Kant condemned theodicy to failure, his most prominent disciple - Hermann Cohen - tried again to corroborate it. Justice, and this applies to divine justice too, is not a descriptive but a normative concept. True justice will be established in the future, but in this world. Man's task is to search for it. For instance, man's physical suffering was intended to awaken the moral feeling of mercy.

> If there has ever been a question of theodicy {...} one might perhaps express its meaning by the paradox: suffering exists on account of mercy. ("*Leiden ist wegen des Mitleids vorhanden.*") [11]

Cohen availed himself of the German word *Mitleid* which literally means "co-suffering".[12] Moreover, suffering is related to forgiveness of sin rather than to sinfulness, but what is most important: Suffering, in particular of the prophet (according to Maimonides, Job was a prophet too), is part of the "theodical organisation of the world"; it does not contradict the world's purposefulness, but expresses the "teleological independence of the moral system".[13] Cohen tries to reintroduce into his rationalist understanding of Judaism some of the beliefs that his mentor had dismissed as incompatible with rational ethical discourse. He reaffirms, in his treatment of justice, the conception of human suffering as part of the divine plan. Even sin is subjected to theodicy because it can be explicated by God's forgiveness. Unless sin, God's mercy would be inconceivable....[14] Hence, suffering is not a punishment, but a revelation of God's justice, combined with his mercy, which together constitute "the principle of divine theodicy".[15] Reason makes us understand that not only individuals suffer for the sake of their fellow beings, but the People of Israel was chosen by divine providence to suffer for the whole of humanity.[16]Leaning on Deutero-Isiah, Cohen asserts that if Israel was chosen for suffering, this cleanses the notion of chosenness from any suspicion of pretentiousness or haughtiness. It corroborates again God's justice. It is only through suffering that moral ideas are manifested. If one were to judge Jewish suffering by eudaemonistic criteria, it is indeed a disaster, but if one interprets it by the "light of theodicy" and the messianic vocation of Israel, it becomes a comprehensible function of Israel's earthly history.[17] Also Leo Baeck, the last chief Rabbi of German Jewry, had expressed about the same time similar ideas in *The Essence of Judaism*. "The best what happened to Israel was given it by suffering."

> Human suffering is a religious good, because and as far as it is able to become a duty. [...] We must also affirm suffering, by transforming it into ethical demand. Do your duty, then also the greatest evil will become beneficent for you. On this agree all the masters and teachers of Israel. For them the question of theodicy has found its answer, or it does not exist at all for them because they apprehend life as a duty".[18]

Would Baeck cling to this optimism, namely that theodicy will ultimately triumph over injustice and evil, after he experienced forty years after having written this, the Holocaust? A. Friedlander, Baeck's biographer, acknowledges that contemporary propositions of theodicy have run into an impasse. This is true of Jewish and Christian theology alike.[19] The same question applies to Cohen. It is difficult to understand how he could reconcile his conception of theodicy with his knowledge of the persecutions, expulsions and martyrdom of the Jewish people during 2000 years of dispersion. Would he have still upheld it after the Holocaust? Though a hypothetical question, it seems unlikely.

Modern philosophical discussions of theodicy

The modern philosophical discussions at theodicy, in general as well as in Jewish thought, focus on three cardinal problems: 1. God's goodness which is incompatible with evil. 2. God's omnipotence which is challenged by the existence of evil. 3. The existence of evil itself. The existence of evil in the world is undeniable. Therefore, the discussion on theodicy considered several aspects of evil: 1. Moral evil whose origin was man. 2. Physical evil, on the one hand disease, pain and suffering, on the other natural disasters as earthquakes, floods, drought and so on. 3. Metaphysical evil, that is the imperfection of created things and beings. Most of the discussions centred on the two first aspects, and resulted in two chief viewpoints: 1. If the source of evil cannot be God, it must be either the devil or man. But the devil (Satan) is, according to the religious tradition of Judaism, only one of God's angels (messengers); therefore it must be man. This, evidently, arouses questions with regard to God's benevolence and omnipotence. Even if he did not create evil, why did he allow for the potential of evil? Moreover, this would also imply that God is not the source of all and everything. Some philosophers, among others Martin Buber, tried to overcome this difficulty by the assertion that evil as such does not exist; it is merely the absence of good.[20] Modern theodicies refused to affirm evil as having a real substance, and therefore employed the language of negation, absence of good and so on. This often involved metaphorical expressions such as "Eclipse" (M. Buber), "Night" (E. Wiesel) or "Death of God" (R. Rubenstein). But nonetheless, evil is ontologically no less real than good. Therefore all attempts to defend God by denying the existence of evil are problematic and unconvincing.

> The Sovereignty of evil has become more real and immediate and familiar than God. The question [...] is not how can God abide evil in the world but how can God be affirmed meaningfully in a world where evil enjoys much dominion.[21]The traditional formulations of theodicy [...] come down particularly hard on the reality of evil.[22]

The theological assumption, endorsed among others already by Maimonides, that God's transcendence prevents any direct relation between him and his creatures after the act of creation, and that he is beyond relation to time, is unconvincing. Biblical tradition gives many examples of God's relation with man in time, such as with Moses, at Mr.Sinai, and so on. A religious philosopher like Maimonides would certainly not deny them either. J.S. Mill and W. James tried to solve the problem by the claim that God is good, but not omnipotent. But such an assertion is obviously unsatisfactory from the theological viewpoint.

2. God created both good and evil, as affirmed already in the Bible. "I make peace and create evil; I the God do all these things." (Isaiah 457 "Good" without its correlative term "evil" would be logically as well as ontologically meaningless. Yet God explicitly ordered man to choose the good. But then again, why did he not create such a world where the other option was ruled out from the beginning? The common answer to this question is that a human being, unable to choose freely between good and evil, would be a mere automaton, that is an imperfect being. He would lack those human features that we value most. Therefore E. Berkovitz tried to interpret Isaiah's statement that God makes peace and creates evil as meaning that God created the possibility of evil, in order to allow for the possibility of its opposite - goodness. Ethics is a human affair, and it is incumbent upon man to realise justice, love, peace, mercy.

> With man the good is axiology; with God, ontology. Man alone can strive and struggle for the good; God is Good. Man alone can create value; God is value.[23]

But how to reconcile this view with the famous Talmudic dictum that he who acts because is he ordered (by God) to do so is greater than he who acts without being ordered?[24] This anticipates in a certain way Kant's moral preference of duty over inclination. So neither of the two attitudes gives a conclusive answer.

If evil is man's fault, namely a consequence of his misuse of the freedom of choice, leading to sinful behaviour, then the evil which befalls him was believed to be divine punishment. God is the God of justice; goodness, benevolence and justice are inseparable elements of his essence. Then whence the suffering of innocents - infants, children? When Abraham argued with God about the fate of Sodom - "Shall not the judge of all the earth do right?" (Genesis 18.25) - God agreed to spare the city if there were ten righteous persons in it. But no mention is made of children. Rather surprisingly, this was passed over in silence by almost all later commentators. None responded as did Dostoevsky's Ivan Karamazov: "There is no justification for the tear of a single suffering child", or A. Camus: "I continue to struggle against this universe in which children suffer and die."[25] Even if one were to accept the distinction between "crime" as the evil behaviour of the individual who alone is responsible and punishable for it, and "sin" as the violation of religious precepts, such as idolatry, for which the whole community is responsible, this does not explain the victimisation of the innocent. Collective punishment is ethically unacceptable. All these theological questions have attained an unprecedented tragic dimension in the wake of the Holocaust. In contemporary Jewish thought one encounters two alternative answers: 1. To protest and to rebel against God; 2. To abandon belief in God.[26] Elie Wiesel, in one of his stories, describes three rabbis who subpoena God to a trial and judge him guilty. E. Berkowitz, E. Fackenheim, R. Rubenstein, three prominent Jewish philosophers to take issue with the Holocaust, reject categorically any attempt to explain it theologically.

God and Evil - the example of Job

Although Jewish tradition interpreted exile and suffering as divine punishment - "Because of our sins, we were exiled from our country" - this is not really what the concept of theodicy stands for. Divine reward and punishment is a reasonable argument of religious belief, whether one accepts it or not. The Talmudic story that "because of Kamza and Bar Kamza Jerusalem was destroyed", exemplifies this attitude.[27] Likewise, the Talmud asks: "Why was the second Temple destroyed? [...] Because of baseless hatred".[28] Moreover, the dissonance between God's justice and the suffering of the virtuous and the well-being of the wicked in this world was explained away either by belief in the afterworld or by eschatological and messianic hopes for a world to come where all these wrongs will be rectified. Despite some current assertions, this is, however, connected to the notion of theodicy only indirectly. Theodicy that explains suffering as punishment is unconvincing with regard to Jewish martyrdom throughout history, and especially after the Holocaust. Theodicy means an unquestioning justification of God's rule in the world which cannot be explained rationally. God does not commend the good because it is good, but whatever God wills or does, is good. Maimonides, discussing divine providence, refuted the adoption of this outlook by the Islamic sect of "Ash'ariyah".[29] Right knowledge of God serves, as it were, as a guarantee against evil. He asserted that the evil which befalls man reflects his insufficient strive for spiritual perfection which alone assures and augments divine providence. However, some of his popular followers inferred from this that a proper understanding of providence inevitably leads to theodicy. Rather unexpectedly, what theodicy ascribes to God, with regard to goodness, Spinoza ascribed to man:

> We do not endeavour, will, seek after or desire because we judge a thing to be good. On the contrary, we judge a thing to be good because we endeavour, will, seek after and desire it.[30]

Many thinkers were struck by the discrepancy between the verse "And God saw everything that he had made, and, behold, it was very good" (Genesis 1:31), and the existence of so much evil in the world. (See above). Some of them tried to overcome this difficulty by the conjecture that "very good" referred only to the ideal state of affairs in the Garden of Eden. "The God-willed perfect world is an exemplary world".[31] That it did not last, was not God's will, but man's fault; but there remains the hope that the ideal state of affairs will return. This was not only the essence of messianic and eschatological beliefs in Judaism and Christianity, but also the crux of

Ernst Bloch's atheistic utopian philosophy of hope. He was fascinated by the problem of theodicy in the wake of the book of "*Job*". It inaugurates the "fatal necessity of theodicy",[32] namely to defend God whose justice is challenged by Job's embarrassing questions: "Wherefore do the wicked live, become old, yes, are mighty in power?" (Job 21.7). Why are the poor hungry? It is not their own fault but the result of their exploitation by the rich, and God does not intervene.

> They also that make the oil within their walls, and tread the wine presses, suffer thirst. Men groan from out of the city, and the soul of the wounded crieth out: yet God layeth not folly to them. (Job 24.11-12)[33]

The unconvincing attempts of the three friends and Elihu to justify God by the banal argument from effect to cause that if there is punishment, there must have been sin, are repudiated by Job straightaway. Moreover, as E. Berkovitz pointed out, by defending the wrong done to Job as justice, they insult the very idea of God in which Job believes. It distorts his concept of God's personage.[34] It ascribes, as it were, to God what Isaiah had accused the wicked among men of: "Woe unto them that call evil good, and good evil. [...] Woe unto them that are wise in their own eyes". (Isaiah 5:20/21) This would be an Orwellian theodicy. But when God himself enters the discussion, he does so without giving any answers. He responds to Job's *moral* questions, concerning the human condition, by rhetorical *physicalist* questions, concerning nature. When Job finally surrenders, he does so not out of being convinced but out of sheer resignation. Similarly, the Talmudic Sage Yannai avowed: "it is not in our power to understand the suffering of the righteous or the well-being of the wicked".[35] He also expressed, though cautiously and indirectly, his malaise of God's rule. Finite man cannot understand, as it were, the will of infinite God. Had Job's "friends" proposed God's cosmological argument, he would not have surrendered and would have continued to insist on the injustice of his undeserved punishment. Theodicy is not vindicated by reason but postulated as part of a theocratic system. (The chapter on Job's reconciliation with God seems to be a later interpolation.)

The successors of Job's three self-righteous friends are the contemporary theologians who still uphold the belief in theodicy after Auschwitz.[36] From the pure philosophical viewpoint the suffering or the death of one innocent person is no less a philosophical problem than the suffering or death of millions of innocents. Nonetheless, if Job's tragic plight puts a question-mark on theodicy - by the way, God himself rebukes the three friends for their simplist apologetic - a *fortiori* the six millionfold extermination of innocents in the *Shoah*. In this vein Buber asked:

How is a life with God still possible in a time in which there is an Auschwitz? [...] Dare we recommend to the survivors of Auschwitz, the Job of the gas-chambers: "Call on Him, for He is kind, for His mercy endureth forever."[37]

In Job's case God at least responded; in the Holocaust he remained silent. Buber tried to propose a partial answer to this unanswerable question by the concept of "*Eclipse of God*" ("*Hester Panim*", *Deus absconditus*), as also did E. Fackenheim and J. Soloweitchik. *Hester Panim* has two meanings: 1. God hides his face from the wicked, and does not prevent the evil that befalls them. (Deut.31:17/18) 2. He hides his face from the innocent, and does not come to their rescue. (Psalm 44).[38] Only the latter concerns theodicy, but it opens a Pandora's box of embarrassing questions: Why did God hide his face? As a punishment? Then for what sins? Of what were six million people, one million of them children, guilty?[39] If, God, according to Buber, can "hide his face" any time, what kind of God does this make of him? How can one justify or love such a God? One seems to turn around in a vicious circle without any outlet.

In the case of Job the assumed theodicy turned into its opposite; it still lacked all the posterior theological and apologetical elements which make it, as it were, inevitable. But since then every theodicy, if it is judged by Job's questions, is mere insincerity.[40] It evokes not only the questionability of God's justice, but of his very existence. Yet the genuine solution of theodicy is not simply the denial of God's existence, but the hope and the rebellion that will ultimately overcome present-day conditions and lay the foundations for the possibility of a just and better world.[41] Theodicy will cede its place to anthropology, in the philosophical sense of the word.

This does not necessarily exclude religious beliefs, as can be learned, among others, from Buber's anthropological inquiries.[42] It is incumbent upon man to realise the yearned-for good. Utopia does not mean impossibility. On the contrary, what is not yet anywhere now - "*u-topos*" - can come into being. This is what Bloch called the "ontology of what is not yet". ("*Ontologie des noch-nicht-Seins*")[43] This is, of course, diametrically opposed to any belief in theodicy.

NOTES

1.Maimonides: *Guide of the Perplexed*, Chicago: Chicago University Press, 1963, Part III, ch.17.

2. Fritz Mauthner: *Woerterbuch der Philosophie*, 2. Band. Zuerich Diogenes, 1980, p.190.

3. S.D.Luzzatto: *Meh'kare ha-Jahadut*, Warsaw, 1913, I, 1, p.11.

4.Immanuel Kant: "Ueber das Misslingen aller philosophischen Versuche in der Theodicee", *Kant's Saemtliche Werke*. Leipzig im Inselverlag, 1921, Vol.4, pp.797-818.

5. *Ibid.*, pp. 799-801.

6. *Ibid.*, pp.802-808. His last assertion is rather surprising because it clashes with his conception of the three transcendental ideas - God, freedom, immortality - which he postulated, in his *Religion in the limits of reason alone* (New York: Harper Torchbooks, 1960), as the foundation of a popular theory of morality. Quite paradoxically, in the essay on theodicy he also rejects what he there accused the Hebrews of lacking namely the belief in immortality which is, as it were, a precondition for a moral theory of reward and punishment.

7. *Ibid.*, p.813.

8.David Hume: *Dialogues concerning Natural Religion*, New York: Social Sciences Publishers, 1948, p.198.

9. It is perhaps noteworthy, and quite surprising, that after all this in France, between 1840 and 1880, theodicy, together with psychology, logic and morality, were the four obligatory subjects of philosophy to be taught in second schools. Andre Lalande: *Vocabulaire technique et critique de la Philosophie*, Paris: Presses Universitaires de France, 1962, p.1124.

10. Already the medieval theologian Petrus Damiani not only allowed for the suspension of ethics by God's will but expressly asserted that if God wills so, even murder becomes ethically valuable. A similar theodician ethics can be found in the philosophy of Duns Scotus. Although God is bound by the logical law of contradiction and the three first commands of the Decalogue, he nevertheless can suspend the ethical independence of those ethical commands that are the most important for man. They depend exclusively on God's will.

11. Hermann Cohen: *Religion of Reason out of the Sources of Judaism*. New York: Frederick Ungar, 1972. The following quotations are from the second German edition: *Religion der Vernunft aus den Quellen des Judentums*. Frankfurt a.M.: Kauffmann Verlag, 1929. *Ibid.*,p.19.

12. Perhaps he was also impressed by S.D.Luzzatto who postulated mercy as one of the three chief elements of Judaism.

13. *Ibid.*, p.265, 267.

14. *Ibid.*, p.243.

15. *Ibid.*, p.502.

16. *Ibid.*, pp.503/3.

17. *Ibid.*,p.312. The invective against eudaemonism reminds one of his hostile attitude to Zionism: "Die Kerle wollen gluecklich sein.....".

18. Quoted from Baeck's *Essence of Judaism* by Albert Friedlander: *Leo Baeck - Leben und Lehre.* Stuttgart: Deutsche Verlagsanstalt, 1973, p.90.

19. Friedlander, *op.cit.*, p.254.

20. Martin Buber: *Images of Good and Evil*, London: Routledge & Kegan Paul, 1952.

21. Arthur A.Cohen: *The Tremendum. A Theological Interpretation of the Holocaust.* New York: Crossroad, 1981, p.34.

22. *Ibid.*,p.48.

23. Eliezer Berkowitz: *Faith after the Holocaust*, New York: Ktav, 1973, p.105.

24. Tractate *Baba Kamma*, 38a.

25. Alber Camus: *Resistance, Rebellion and Death*, New York: Knopf, 1961, p.71. See also David Birnbaum: *God and Evil, a Jewish Perspective*, Hoboken, NJ: Ktav, 1989, p.4.

26. Goethe recounted in his autobiography *Dichtung und Wahrheit* that the earthquake in Lisbon caused him to lose his belief in God. If this terrible disaster which played also an important role in Voltaire's *Candid*, evoked such a response from the young Goethe, *a fortiori* the tremendous unprecedented Holocaust from contemporary thinkers.

27. Tractate *Gittin* 55b-56a. On the story in the *Aggadah* that served as background to this proclamation, see *Encyclopedia Judaica*, Jerusalem: Keter, 1971, vol.10, p.732.

28. Tractate *Yoma* 9b.

29. *Guide of the Perplexed, op cit.*, III, 17 (see note 1).

30. Baruch Spinoza: *The Ethics*, III, prop. 9, Scholium.

31. Michael Landmann: *Ursprungsbild Schoepfertat - Zum platonisch-biblischen Gespraech.* Muenchen: Nymphenburger Verlagshandlung, 1966, p.171.

32. Ernst Bloch: *Atheismus im Christentum - Zur Religion des Exodus und des Reichs.* Frankfurt a.M.: Suhrkamp, 1968. p.150.

32

33. *Ibid.*

34. Berkovitch, *op.cit.*, p.68.

35. Tractate *Abot*, 4:14.

36. Bloch, *op cit.*, p.158.

37. M.Buber: *The Dialogue between Heaven and Earth*, quoted by Birnbaum, *op.cit.*, p.11.

38. Berkovitz, *op.cit.*, p.95.

39. Birnbaum, *ibid.*, pp.130/1.

40. Bloch, *op.cit.*, pp.161/3.

41. Ernst Bloch: "Grundrisse einer besseren Welt". *Das Prinzip Hoffnung*, Frankfurt a.M.: Suhrkamp, 1959, 4. Teil, pp.523-1086. See Ze'ev Levy: "Utopia and Reality in the Philosophy of Ernst Bloch", *Utopian Studies*, Vol.1, No.2, 1990, pp.3-12.

42. Martin Buber: "Das Problem des Menschen", "Beitraege zu einer philosophischen Anthropologie", *Werke*. Heidelberg: Lambert Schneider, 1962, pp.307-502. *Paths in Utopia*, London: Routledge & Kegan Paul, 1949, *Eclipse of God. Studies in the Relation between Religion and Philosophy*. New York: Harper & Brothers, 1952, London: Gollancz 1953. *Images of Good and Evil. Op.cit.*

43. Ernst Bloch: "Zur Ontologie des Noch-Nicht-seins". *Tuebinger Einleitung in die Philosophie*. Frankfurt a.M: Suhrkamp, 1970, pp.212-242.

Chapter III

THEODICY AND ANTI-THEODICY IN BIBLICAL AND RABBINIC LITERATURE

Marvin Fox

The Philosophical Problem

In ordinary human experience we find almost no connection between virtue and happiness. The apparently wildly random distribution of pain or prosperity, the seeming arbitrariness of human destiny, is thought by many to be one of the strongest of all challenges to religious faith. It is widely taught that, according to the doctrine of the biblically based religions, God is all-powerful and all-good. Presumably, then, He should be able to prevent unmerited human suffering. The standard philosophical formulation of the puzzle is familiar to everyone who deals with this problem. Given God's power and His benevolence, how is it possible that there is evil in the world. If He wants to prevent it, but is unable, then His power is limited. if He is able, but does not choose to prevent it, then He is not good. Either way, the argument goes, standard religious claims about God are refuted.

This approach of some philosophers to the problem is countered by other philosophical arguments that try to justify God by introducing a variety of qualifications into the argument. These range from the claim that evil is a form of non-being and is thus purely illusory, to highly complex efforts to show that God has morally sufficient reasons for permitting evil to exist in the world, to the argument that God is limited in power and cannot fully control events. Typically, the philosophic treatments of this subject are carried on from a position that is external to the community of religious faith. The philosophers, for the most part, seem to have no personal stake in the outcome of the investigation. They are merely dealing with one more interesting technical problem that presents them with an intellectual challenge.

Biblical Responses

The approach to the problem from within the life of religious faith is, in certain respects, radically different because it is characterised by passionate involvement. This is especially evident in the Bible and in rabbinic literature where we find uncompromising faith in divine justice balanced by anguished concern to understand God's mysterious ways. Sometimes the answers are easy to come by, in particular when there seems to be a direct correlation between sin and punishment. Adam knows why he is condemned to exile from paradise and to a life of toil, since God tells him explicitly that it is because he ate of the forbidden fruit.[1] Noah is told that God has "decided to put an end to all flesh, for the earth is filled with lawlessness because of them: I am about to destroy them with the earth".[2] Similarly, Abraham, despite his challenge to God, knows finally that God is acting justly in His destruction of Sodom and Gomorra. As God say, their "outrage is so great, and their sin so grave"[3] that they must be destroyed.

At other times there is no answer readily available and suffering generates bitter complaint, even challenge to God, but hardly ever at the expense of continuing faith and trust. Jeremiah openly challenges God to a trial, knowing in advance that He will prevail. "You will win, O Lord, if I make a claim against You, yet I shall present charges against You: Why does the way of the wicked prosper? Why are the workers of treachery at ease?"[4] Even his bitter certainty that he will receive no answer does not weaken the prophet's faith in God and in His justice. The classical biblical case, of course, is that of Job who in his bitterness proclaims, "Though I were blameless, He would prove me crooked...It is all one; therefore I say, 'He destroys the blameless and the guilty'."[5]

In these few passages, which are a small selection from many such, we see that in the Bible we already have both theodicy and anti-theodicy as widely present counter-elements. Human suffering is often explained as a direct consequence of sin. We violate God's commandments and He punishes us. This simple explanation is opposed by challenges, even attacks, on God because there appears to be so much unjust and unearned human suffering. Job's friends offer the easy answer; he must have sinned grievously to have received such punishment. Yet Job himself never yields on this point, insisting that he is not guilty and demanding a trial. In the end, as we know, he does not receive a specific justification of his suffering, but yet he responds in humble faith as he submits to the divine decree. What is most instructive is that God condemns Job's friends, saying to them, "you have not spoken the truth about Me as did My servant Job".[6] This suggests to us that God himself does not approve of those attempts at theodicy which reduce very complex questions to unacceptably simple answers and try to dispel the mysterious darkness with an artificial light that obscures more than it illuminates. It seems that in God's eyes, faith and trust, however troubled, are preferable to false or tendentious apologetics. As is often said in traditional circles of talmudic learning, not every question must be answered, nor must every puzzle be resolved.

Responses in Earlier Rabbinic Literature

The same two tendencies are present in rabbinic literature. We frequently find easy justifications of God which are just as frequently countered by a recognition of our inability to justify His ways in the world. Moses, the greatest of the prophets, is represented in the Talmud as asking God to explain why the righteous suffer and the wicked prosper. He wants desperately to understand how God works in human history. According to one view, his question was answered, although in a way that is far from satisfying. Moses was taught that the righteous man who suffers is the son of a wicked man, while the wicked man who prospers is the son of a righteous man. The one is apparently paying for his father's sins, while the other is the beneficiary of his father's virtue. This explanation is then modified by the assertion that the righteous man who suffers is imperfect in his righteousness, while the wicked man who prospers is not absolutely wicked.[7] It is self-evident that this explanation fails to give us a justification for God's actions. It is not clear at all why one who is mostly, although not perfectly, righteous should have a lower standing than one who is mostly, but not absolutely, wicked.

According to a second view, Moses received no answer at all. Rabbi Meir teaches that God turned down Moses's request for enlightenment by affirming that He acts as He chooses. "For it is said: 'And I will be gracious to whom I will be gracious', although he may not deserve it, 'And I will show mercy on whom I will show mercy', although he may not deserve it."[8] One should not misconstrue this statement to mean that R. Meir was asserting that God behaves in ways that are purely arbitrary or capricious. All he is saying is that we are not capable of giving a full and satisfactory account of God's ways in the world. God makes His own decisions on grounds that are known to Him, but we humans cannot and need not justify His ways. Our stance should be the stance of faithful trust in His justice and benevolence. This same position is set forth in the well-known story of Moses being transported forward in time to the lecture hall of R. Akiba. Having discovered the latter's remarkable greatness and creativity in understanding the Torah, Moses asks God to show him the reward that awaits the sage. When Moses sees the martyrdom of R. Akiba and its aftermath, he cries out bitterly, "Lord of the Universe, such Torah and such a reward!" To which God replies, "Be silent, for such is My decree".[9] Here again Moses is left without insight into God's ways, while he is challenged at the same time not to question, not to doubt, but to maintain his faith in God's justice and benevolence.

It is characteristic of rabbinic literature that these antithetical approaches to the problem of evil are found side by side, often within a single text. We shall see that this is true of both the earlier and later levels of that literature. Let us consider first some tannaitic sources. In a well-known text R. Yannai teaches that "the tranquillity of the wicked and the suffering of the righteous" are both "beyond our grasp".[10] The exact meaning of *ein bevadenu* is not absolutely clear. However, the classical commentators illustrate our point by offering two main lines of interpretation. One asserts that we simply do not understand God's ways, while the other justifies God by explaining this passage to mean that we do not see His Justice in this world only because all will be rectified in the world-to-come. Both are agreed in taking for granted that, whether we understand human destiny or not, God is just.

In Sifre Deuteronomy[11] we find a striking instance of this dual approach. The passage is a midrashic exposition of the verse, "The Rock!- His deeds are perfect, yea, all His ways are just; a faithful God, never false, true and upright is He". (Deuteronomy 32.4) Clearly this verse presents a challenge to anyone concerned with theodicy, and the midrash responds to that challenge. The initial response consists simply of a strong assertion that God's work is, in fact, perfect and His ways are just, however it may appear to us, and it is improper for us to question, to complain, or to try to explain His ways. This anti-theodicy by affirmation without explanation is followed by a standard justification of the apparent failure to reward the righteous and punish the wicked in this world. We are assured that all the seeming injustice in apportioning rewards in this world will be set right in the future judgement to which we shall all be subjected in the next world. There God "will sit in judgement on each one and give him what is appropriate for him". The wicked are rewarded in this world for whatever minor righteous deeds they performed, so that they may then be punished in the next world for all their evil deeds. In turn, the righteous are punished in this world for their minor transgressions so that they may receive the full reward for their virtue in the world-to-come. God's justice is absolute, but we fail to see it here since it is carried out fully only in the hereafter. Anti-theodicy and conventional theodicy live in this passage side by side. So far does the conventional theodicy go in this passage that it concludes by describing for us the procedure which will be followed in the final judgement. Each person, we are told will be presented with an exact accounting of all his deeds on earth. He will be required to verify the account and to sign it as evidence that he acknowledges the absolute justice of God's verdict.

In the last step the passage then teaches that here on earth we must accept without complaint whatever is meted out to us, because only in this way do we demonstrate our faith in divine justice and perfection. The model is that of the great sage R. Haninah ben Teradion, his wife and his daughter. The parents are condemned to a martyr's death, and the daughter is reduced from her exalted station and assigned to work in a brothel. Yet, no word of complaint is recorded. Instead, the sage and his wife justify God while reciting portions of the verse we are expounding. The daughter similarly justifies God while reciting another verse (Jeremiah 32:19). As the midrash text puts, "The three directed their hearts (towards God) and accepted the justice of God's judgement". Here we are presented with the recurring model of true faith. Men and women who have committed themselves to the truth of the Torah and have lived meticulously by its teachings accept even the most horrible fate with equanimity because they are confident that God acts righteously. What is especially instructive is that R. Haninah and his family accept their fate without attempting to offer any explanation of why it is just or how they will be compensated for their suffering. In contrast, the text introduces a philosopher (who is clearly a non-Jew) who admires and praises the faithful martyrs. When he too is condemned to death by the authorities he rejoices because, "tomorrow my portion will be with them in the world to come". Note that the philosopher is driven to provide a theodicy, namely, the assurance that his suffering will be amply compensated in the world-to-come. For him faith must somehow be supplemented by a reassuring argument.

A final tannaitic example will show us how far the ancient sages were prepared to go in pursuing theodicy and anti-theodicy side by side. One of the great moments in biblical history in which God's power is openly exercised to save His people is the splitting of the Sea of Reeds. After the children of Israel have safely crossed over and their pursuers are drowned, Moses leads the people in a hymn of glorification, proclaiming God's might and His saving power. "I will sing to the Lord, for He has triumphed gloriously; horse and driver He has hurled into the sea."[12]

Throughout the song God is exalted and praised. The climax seems to be reached when He is proclaimed to be above all other beings who claim some divine status. "Who is like You, O Lord among the celestials [*ba-elim*], who is like You, majestic in holiness, awesome in splendour, working wonders."[13] These words of pure praise seem clear and unambiguous. Yet there is at least one tannaitic exposition of this text which construes it to have a vastly different meaning.[14]

The first comments on this verse are conventional variations on the basic theme which stresses God's power as it manifested itself by saving the Israelites and destroying the idolaters. This thrust reaches its height when the term "*ba-elim*" is read as "*ba-alamim*" i.e., those with vast power. The midrash now construes the verse in the following way: "Who is like unto Thee among the strong and who is like unto Thee in the wonders and mighty deeds which Thou didst perform at the sea".[15]

Remarkably, the very next words reverse completely the mood of praise in favour of seeming doubt and bitterness, and they do so with a play on the same key term. Now "*ba-elim*" is read as "*ba-ilmim*" and the whole verse is turned on its head. The highest praise becomes the most bitter condemnation. Not who is like you, O Lord, in the whole pantheon of those who claim to be divine beings, who has your power and your devotion to those who serve you? Instead the verse is now read, "Who is like You among the silent [mute], O Lord. Who like You sees the degradation of your children and remains silent [doing nothing to save them]?" God is here accused of apparent indifference to the bitter fate of His chosen people. His one time power exercised against the oppressors of the Israelites, is now held back in restrained silence. This text reflects the reality of later Jewish history in which the people often suffered bitterly at the hands of power enemies, while God remained silent, refusing to intervene to save them. If the first interpretation of our verse is theodicy at its most impressive, this later interpretation is equally forceful anti-theodicy. No explanation or justification is given for God's silence, just the almost laconic statement of the fact. This is no denial of faith, only a denial that we can give an account of God's action or inaction which is fully consistent with our understanding of His nature and of the biblical promises.[16]

Responses in Later Rabbinic Literature

This same combination of theodicy and anti-theodicy is present as well in the later rabbinic materials, in the Gemara and in the post-tannaitic midrashim. Our space permits us to examine only a few examples. R. Ammi teaches that there is no death without sin and no suffering without iniquity.[17]He offers a simple and familiar explanation of the painful aspects of human experience. Our suffering is punishment for our transgressions of God's commandments, and our very mortality is the consequence of our sinfulness. However, instead of accepting this easy theodicy, the text goes on to refute it by considering a variety of cases which do not fit this model. The discussion concludes with anti-theodicy, stating that we have proof that "there is death without sin and suffering without iniquity. Thus the refutation of R. Ammi is [indeed] a refutation".[18] As in the other cases we have studied, we see here a rejection of easy answers to hard questions. The Sages had no problem about admitting that they could not give a fully satisfactory account of the phenomenon of human suffering.

An even more striking instance occurs in an extended discussion which introduces the concept of *yissurin shel ahavah*, suffering which is a mark of God's special love. As Rava puts it, "If the Holy One, blessed be He, is pleased with a man, he crushes him with painful sufferings".[19] Rashi explains the concept of *yissurin shel ahavah* in the following way: "The Holy One, blessed be He, causes suffering to a person in this world, even though that person is without sin, in order to increase his reward in the world-to-come beyond that which he strictly merits".[20] In the discussion which follows this justification of the suffering of the righteous is defended and explicated with various prooftexts and is refined in a number of ways. One view is that not only are these sufferings the prologue to great reward in the hereafter, but they also assure one that his children will have long life and that his Torah learning will never leave him. To guard against this explanation not working out, another view is introduced. "If a man busies himself in the study of Torah and in acts of charity and [nonetheless] buries his children, all his sins are forgiven him."[21] It seems that it is always possible, with sufficient determination and ingenuity, to find a satisfactory explanation of even the most painful human experiences. If one explanation goes contrary to actual events, another can be produced to cover the new situation.

It is against this form of theodicy that Antony Flew argued so vigorously in the famous "Theology and Falsification" debate. Flew makes the point that "if there is nothing which a putative assertion denies then there is nothing which it asserts either: and so it is not really an assertion".[22]Flew concludes his discussion with a challenge to religious believers. "What would have to occur or to have occurred to constitute for you a disproof of the love of, or of the existence of, God?" The answer seems to be that nothing can shake the faithful in their conviction that God is just, no set of events is sufficient to falsity the theodicy of the faithful. As we have seen, one can always provide an explanation or justification of human suffering, even that of the most virtuous. Moreover, if one explanation does not work, there is always another readily available. Once we claim to know God's ways in the world, we can always provide an account which defends Him against charges of injustice or lack of power or benevolence.

Yet, even in the talmudic passage concerning chastisement of love which we have been examining, there is also an anti-theodicy element. Sages of unquestioned standing and unquestioned piety reject for themselves the seeming attractions of suffering in this world so as to merit great reward in the world-to-come. The passage concludes by recounting several episodes involving some of the greatest figures of the age. In each case the sage has fallen ill and is suffering. A colleague visits him, and in the course of the visit asks, "Are your sufferings pleasing [havivin] to you?" One would expect a positive answer, since such suffering is thought to be evidence of God's special love and the great reward which it guarantees in the next world. Yet, in each case the sage replies, "Neither they nor their reward". At this point the visitor takes his hand and cures him of his illness.[23] We see here forceful anti-theodicy expressed not as theological theory, but as actually practised in the lives of great scholars who are models of piety and learning. They reject outright the theodicy of "sufferings of love" and find no comfort in the idea that their pain in this world will be compensated by great rewards in the hereafter. The Talmud has no problem about setting antithetical views side by side, recognising that there is a legitimate place both for theodicy and the denial of theodicy within the Jewish tradition. What matters is that in Job-like fashion those who reject the various efforts at theodicy remain fully within the community of faith, no less than those who accept conventional theodicy as their doctrine.

This tension between theodicy and anti-theodicy shows up again in the interpretation of a mishna by a later sage. The mishna teaches that whoever fulfils a single divine commandment is assured of reward. "Good is done to him, he is assured of long life, and he inherits an assured place in the world-to-come".[24] This seemingly extravagant claim is tempered by the discussion in the gemara that follows. It is qualified to mean that when a man's record is evenly balanced between good deeds and evil deeds, the addition of one more good deed tips the scale in his favour and assures him of divine reward. However, even this hypothesis is questioned on the ground that there is a teaching (which we discussed above) that the virtuous suffer in this world so that they may collect their full reward in the next world, and the reverse with regard to the wicked. This finally leads to the theodicy of R. Jacob that, "We receive no reward in this world for the commandments which we fulfill". Only in the world-to-come are we finally rewarded for our virtuous behaviour.[25]

What moved R. Jacob to assign all reward to the next world was his experience of the seeming arbitrariness of human destiny in this world. He provides us with a classic model. There are two commandments in the Torah for whose observance long life is promised. One is honouring parents, and the other is sending away the mother bird before taking eggs or chick from her nest.[26] Yet R. Jacob reports a case in which a father asks his son to climb up to the loft and bring down some young birds. Obeying his father, the son climbs up, sends away the mother bird, and takes the young birds. On his way down, he falls to his death, despite his explicit fulfilment of the two commandments that promise the reward of long life. This reinforces R. Jacob's view that there are no rewards in this life, only in the world-to-come. Clearly this is a paradigm of all simple theodicy. Whatever happens to a man in this world, we can be certain that it will all be set right in the next. if this is true even for those commandments which seem to promise long life in this world, how much more so for those that have no such promise attached to them. It is an act of faith to affirm, with whatever prooftexts one can muster, that God is just and benevolent, but that we do not see his justice or compassion in this worldly life. R.Jacob, it is noted, was the grandson of the great apostate sage, Elisha ben Abuyah (known as Aher, "the other"), whose apostasy was caused by witnessing apparent divine injustice and being unable to account for it. If he had understood the biblical promises of long life as his grandson did, Aher, we are assured, "would not have sinned".[27]

Yet all this strenuous effort at theodicy is rejected by a single prosaic comment in this same passage. An anonymous participant in the discussion evades all the theological puzzles by noting that the obedient son was imprudent and climbed up to the loft on a rickety ladder. No wonder that it collapsed and he fell to his death. The whole event is construed in purely natural terms. The text adds the observation that in dangerous circumstances where injury is to be expected we don't reply on miracles to save us. The young man was responsible for his own death because of his carelessness, and it is utterly inappropriate to expect God to intervene miraculously to save him. Even with divine promises of long life to assure us, we should never tempt fate. Again theodicy is balanced by anti-theodicy.

We cannot conclude this brief study without considering what is perhaps the most instructive anti-theodicy text in the whole rabbinic corpus. I refer to Leviticus Rabbah, Chapter 20,[28] where there is a long meditation on the implications of the death of Nadav and Avihu, the two sons of Aaron the High Priest. In the scriptural account we are simply told that at the consecration of the sanctuary in the desert they offered up a strange fire which God had not commanded. As a consequence, they were immediately consumed by fire. The midrash addresses the puzzling question as to why these two young men should have met such a violent death. What kind of divine justice was it that punished them so severely for a seemingly minor infraction?

Some sections of this long midrashic exegesis deal with the problem through conventional theodicy. In these discussions the death of Nadav and Avihu is understood as the inevitable consequence of their sinfulness. The range of their supposed improprieties is represented as broad and severe. They are supposed to have been deeply disrespectful to their father and to Moses, their uncle. They presumed to teach and to decide questions of law in the presence of Moses their teacher.[29] Walking behind Moses and Aaron, they said to each other, "When will these two old men finally die so that we can assume the leadership of the community?"[30] So great was their arrogance that they dwelt constantly on their aristocratic family connections and considered that there were no women worthy to be their wives.[31] They were guilty of a variety of ritual violations for which the death penalty is ordained.[32] Although there is almost nothing in the biblical text to support these charges, they serve one important purpose, namely, to show us that God does not punish arbitrarily. Here we have conventional theodicy operating in its usual way.

The other side of this same midrash, however, rejects out of hand these efforts to explain and justify God. Instead they depict Nadav and Avihu as men of exemplary virtue, and they show God lamenting the tragedy of their death. They were guilty, according to this version of only one sin, namely the improper fire which they brought to the altar. It is difficult for the midrashic authors to understand why this one sin should have weighed so heavily against all their virtues, and they make it a special point to underscore those virtues. "R. Elazar ha-Moda'i taught: Come and see how difficult the death of the sons of Aaron was for God. Whenever He mentions their death, He mentions their [one] sin. He goes to such trouble in order to deny any ground on which to claim that they died because of evil deeds that they committed secretly."[33] In fact, we are told, so virtuous and beloved were they that God grieved over their death twice as much as their father did.[34]

The theme of anti-theodicy is forcefully introduced at the very beginning of this midrashic passage. Referring to the death of the two sons of Aaron, the text cites Ecclesiastes, 9:2 which sets the tone for much of what follows. "For the same fate is in store for all: for the righteous, and for the wicked; for the good and pure, and for the impure........" This sceptical rejection of conventional theodicy is then amplified by a series of examples. They show that, according to the scriptural account, exactly the same fate awaited paragons of virtue and models of vice. Moses, the virtuous, spoke only in praise of the land of Israel, while the faithless spies denigrated the land. Yet both were equally denied entry into the land. Nebuchadnezzar, who destroyed the Temple, reigned as long as David, who planned and laid the foundations for the Temple. Wicked Korah and his band were burned to death, and the righteous sons of Aaron were also burned to death.[35] Perhaps the most devastating parallel is drawn between Titus the oppressor and Nadav and Avihu, priests in the service of God. "Wicked Titus entered the Holy of Holies [where only the High Priest was permitted to enter] with his unsheathed sword in hand. He cut the hanging over the Holy Ark and his sword was covered with blood. Yet he entered in peace and came out in peace [i.e., he was unscathed]. In contrast, the sons of Aaron entered the sanctuary to present offerings to God, and they were carried out having been burned to death."[36] Where then is divine justice? Ecclesiastes seems to be correct when he argues that the same fate awaits the righteous and the wicked. In fact, the wicked seem sometime to be rewarded, while the righteous are condemned to suffering.

So far does this anti-theodicy go that it argues that it is utterly mistaken for us to expect joy and pleasure in our lives. God is represented as depicting the fate of great figures in early biblical history. Of each of them He says that they had no joy in God's world, why then should any of the rest of us expect lives of joy? The text lists Adam, Abraham, the people of Israel, all of whom experienced sorrow rather than joy. In a stunning climax the text concludes, "The Holy One, blessed, be He, had no joy in His world, why then do you expect to live in happiness?".[37] The straightforward theodicy which explains the death of Aaron's sons as a consequence of their very grave sins is here rejected out of hand. They were righteous men, but like other righteous men there is no connection between their virtue and their destiny. Perhaps we shall one day be able to get beyond the sceptical bitterness of Ecclesiastes and come to understand God's ways in the world, but for now we can only note the dark mystery. Even Ecclesiastes ends on a note of pious submission to the Almighty, and a confident assertion that we shall all be called to account for our deeds.

This reluctance to explain God's ways when we have no satisfactory explanations, this anti-theodicy, is validated in a talmudic discussion which is luminous in its clarity. The Sages noted that Moses instituted a standard way of speaking in praise of God. He described Him as "great, mighty, and awesome",[38] a formula which is used to this day in the statutory liturgy. Yet, despite the authority of Moses, the Talmud notes, Jerimiah and Daniel each dropped one adjective from this formula. Jeremiah spoke of God only as "great and Mighty" and Daniel spoke of Him only as "great and awesome".[39] These omissions are explained as protests against God's failure to protect His sanctuary and His people. "Jeremiah came and said, 'Aliens are dancing wildly in His temple. Where are His awesome deeds?' Daniel came and said, 'Aliens are enslaving His children. Where are His mighty deeds"?[40] The prophets refused to praise God in ways which did not comport with the reality that they experienced. They did not abandon their faith, or even their confidence in His justice and compassion. Nevertheless, if the Temple was destroyed and the people forced to serve a foreign potentate in exile from their land, Jeremiah and Daniel were unwilling to praise God as awesome or mighty. These are protests of anti-theodicy now attributed to the most elevated leaders of the people of Israel. If God seems to have withdrawn from history, they are saying, we will not justify Him with empty praise. Most illuminating is the conclusion of the discussion. The question is raised, how could even these great prophets reject a formula instituted by Moses. The answer given by the Talmud is that, "Since they knew that the Holy One, blessed be He, is Himself committed to truth, they refused to speak falsely of Him".[41] This is a majestic anti-theodicy, one which is motivated by faith and trust in God, and by the conviction that we are not called on, nor are we qualified to defend Him.

A Halakhic Conclusion

I believe that this is the point underlying a halakha universally accepted in traditional circles. A mishna rules that we are obligated to praise God for the bad things that happen to us, just as we must praise him for the good.[42] This teaches us that Judaism rejects Gnostic or metaphysical dualism. With Isaiah, the tradition affirms that there is only one God who must be understood as responsible for all existence, for the good and the bad.[43] Or as it is put in Lamentations, "Is it not at the word of the Most High, that weal and woe befall"?[44] This affirmation that God is the source of both "weal and woe" does not entail simple or conventional theodicy, although that is certainly one legitimate option. The requirement to praise God for the bad just as we do for the good puts upon the community of faith the responsibility to acknowledge that all that happens comes from God. Whether it is pleasant or painful, it is understood as carrying a divine imprimatur, and thus imposes on us the duty to accept whatever God determines as our lot. We may protest. We may rebel. We may question. We need not, however, seek easy answers. Anti-theodicy, when accompanied by a blessing for *dayyan emet*. the true judge, is a stance of faith which Judaism affirms as no less authentic than that of theodicy.

NOTES

1. Genesis 3:17-19. Unless otherwise noted, all biblical quotations are from the NJPS translation.

2. Genesis 6:11-13.

3. Genesis 18:20-22.

4. Jeremiah 12:1.

5. Job 9: 20-22.

6. Job 42:7.

7. b.Berakhot 7a.

8. Ibid. In translating passages from the Babylonian Talmud, I follow the Soncino version with occasional minor adjustments.

9. b.Menahot 29b.

48

10. M.Avot 4:15.

11. Sifre Deuteronomy, Piska 307, ed.Finkelstein, pp.344-346: translated by Reuven Hammer. (Yale University Press, 1986) pp.310-313.

12. Exodus 15: 1.

13. Ibid, 15:11.

14. The discussion which follows is taken from Mekhilta de-Rabbi Yishmael, Treatise Shirata, Chapter 8: Horovitz-Rabin edition, p.142; Lauterbach edition, Vol.2, p.60.

15. Lauterbach translation.

16. It is important to note that the Mekhilta text follows the passage we quoted with a prooftext from Isaiah 42:14-15. If these verses are read in the context of the entire chapter, they may be construed as a kind of justification. God's silence is a consequence of the sins of the people of Israel.

17. b.Shabbat 55a.

18. Ibid.,55b.

19. b.Berakhot 5a.

20. Ibid., s.v. *yissurin shel ahavah.*

21. Ibid., 5ab.

22. Antony Flew. "Theology and Falsification", *New Essays in Philosophical Theology*, Antony Flew and Alisdair Macintyre, eds., (SCM Press Ltd., London, 1963), pp.96-99.

23. b.Berakhot 5b.

24. M.Kiddushin 1:10.

25. For this discussion see b.Kiddushin 39b.

26. See Exodus 19:12, Deuteronomy 5:16 for honouring parents, and Deuteronomy 22:7 for sending away the mother bird.

27. b.Kiddushin 39b.

28. See Vayyikra Rabbah ed.Mordecai Margulies, (Jerusalem, 1972), Parashah 20, Vol.1, pp.441-472. For a listing of parallel texts see the first footnote of each section in this edition. Our summaries sometimes follow the text of a variant reading listed by Margulies, as preferable.

29. Ibid., Sec.6.

30. Ibid.,Sec.10.

31. Ibid.

32. Ibid.,Secs.8,9.

33. Ibid., Sec.8.

34. Ibid., Sec.10.

35. Ibid.,Sec.1.

36. Ibid.,Sec.5.

37. Ibid., Sec.2. The statement quoted about God begins with the qualification, *keveyakhol*, that is to say, if we may be allowed to speak of God in human terms.

38. Deuteronomy 10:17.

39. Jeremiah 33:18; Daniel 9:4.

40. b.Yoma 69b.

41. Ibid. On the statement that God is "*amiti*", Rashi comments, "He affirms the truth and hates falsehood".

42. M.Berakhot 9:5. For a more extended discussion of this theme see M.Fox, "The Unity and Structure of Rabbi Joseph B.Soloveitchik's Thought", *Tradition* 24 (2), 1989, pp.49-55.

43. Isaiah 45:6,7.

44. Lamentations 3:38.

Chapter IV

TISH'AH B'AV AND THE INTERPRETATION OF SUFFERING
Theodore Weinberger

There is a famous midrash on the first verse of Numbers 14. The Israelites have just heard the report of the spies, who spoke of the land of Israel as "one that devours its settlers" (13.32). In response, "the whole community broke into loud cries, and the people wept that night" (14.1). The midrash says that "that night" was the ninth of Av (*Tish'ah B'Av*),[1] and that after hearing the people's cries, God tells them: "Since you have cried needlessly on this night, I will establish this as a night of crying for generations" (see *Ta'anit 29a*). One way of reading this midrash is to say that in the future God will establish *Tish'ah B'Av* as a night of crying- with the destruction of the two Jerusalem Temples (said to occur on the ninth day of Av in 586 BCE and 70 CE, respectively). Indeed, based upon the way *Tish'ah B'Av* is generally observed, one could say that this is the normative reading of this midrash, for the focus in the observance of *Tish'ah B'Av* is on commemorating the anniversaries of the destruction of the Temples. There is another way of reading this midrash, however; and that is to suggest that on the very night that the Israelites cried, God fully establishes *Tish'ah B'Av* as a night for crying. From that night on, every *Tish'ah B'Av* would be an occasion to feel and think deeply about suffering. Viewed in this way, the destructions of the Temples do not establish the essential nature of the day- they were horrific incarnations of this day of crying.

This paper focuses on *Tish'ah B'Av* in its larger context as a day set aside for crying. I will look at resources in the Jewish tradition that encourage Jews to feel and think about *Tish'ah B'Av* as a day of ritualised suffering, a day to contemplate how suffering occurs and why it occurs. It should be noted at the outset, however, that most Jews who use these resources, that is most Jews who observe *Tish'ah B'Av*, are Orthodox. The experiences of *Tish'ah B'Av* described in this paper are thus experiences associated with Orthodox Judaism (the branch of Judaism with which I affiliate communally but not theologically). Of course, my depiction of *Tish'ah B'Av* as more than a day commemorating the destruction of the Temples tacitly encourages more observance of *Tish'ah B'Av* in the Jewish community.[2] Whereas just Orthodox Jews pray for a return of the Temple and of animal sacrifice, all human beings know of suffering. A wider appropriation of *Tish'ah B'Av* could only serve for spiritual enrichment.

Ezekiel 24 and Ritualised Suffering

Tish'ah B'Av is publicly commemorated in the same manner that an individual mourns. Just as an individual is to go into ritual mourning at the death of an immediate family member, so the Jewish community is instructed to ritually mourn the loss of the two Temples. A major source for this linkage of public and private mourning is Ezekiel 24, where Ezekiel's suffering at the loss of his wife is designed to be emblematic of the impending suffering of the Jews at the loss of the Temple. The mourning practices of Ezekiel prefigure the suffering of the Jews, and the Rabbis in turn utilize Ezekiel's practices to commemorate the suffering. A key lesson to be learned here is that suffering teaches about suffering; that is, the suffering of Ezekiel at the death of his wife is to inform the Jews' subsequent suffering at the destruction of the Temple and of Jerusalem.

The occasion for Chapter 24 of Ezekiel is the beginning of Babylon's siege of Jerusalem (in January of 588 BCE).[3] Ezekiel's immediate audience are those Jews who, like himself, already live in Babylon (many were exiled in 598 at the time of Babylonian King Nebuchadnezzar's first attack on Judah). God says to Ezekiel: "O mortal, I am about to take away the delight of your eyes from you through pestilence, but you shall not lament or weep or let your tears flow. Moan softly; observe no mourning for the dead: Put on your turban and put your sandals on your feet; do not cover over your upper lip, and do not eat the bread of comforters" (24.16-17).[4] Ezekiel's wife dies that evening, and the people, surprised that Ezekiel does not mourn his wife, ask: "Will you not tell us what these things portend for us, that you are acting so?" (24.19). Ezekiel replies that God has said: "I am going to desecrate My Sanctuary, your pride and glory, the delight of your eyes and the desire of your heart; and the sons and daughters you have left behind [in Judah] shall fall by the sword. And Ezekiel shall become a portent for you: you shall do just as he has done, when it happens; and you shall know that I am the Lord God" (24.21, 24).[5] To underscore matters, Ezekiel adds: "Accordingly, you shall do as I have done: you shall not cover over your upper lips or eat the bread of comforters; and your turbans shall remain on your heads, and your sandals upon your feet. You shall not lament or weep, but you shall be heartsick because of your iniquities and shall moan to one another". Although Ezekiel's words here provide the people with little hope or comfort, they will be useful to the Jews in the days ahead. These words will allow the people a chance to make sense of their suffering because it is through their suffering that they will know their "Lord God". And how are they to know this? Because "Ezekiel shall become a portent"; his suffering is to provide the interpretive key for the people's suffering. The people are to suffer as Ezekiel suffers, and they are to trust in God as Ezekiel trusts in God. Though, because of their sins, the Jews will not be allowed the customary ritual outlet for their suffering, they will be able to make sense of their suffering. And if we remember that Ezekiel's message here is from God (who chooses words with care), we can go on to say that it is *precisely* the suffering of Ezekiel that could get the people to know the "Lord God". The people are only able to interpret their suffering through the suffering of Ezekiel.

Ezekiel 24 does not provide any meaning for suffering from a standpoint outside of suffering. It suggests that if one wants to learn from one's own suffering, then one should look at the suffering of another. The rabbis implemented the obverse corollary to this lesson when it came time to commemorate the destruction of the

54

Temples. They found that it is easier to learn from and about the suffering of *others* when one is in a position of some kind of suffering oneself. In effect, therefore, the practices they institute for *Tish'ah B'Av* constitute ritualized suffering. The Jewish people are to suffer on *Tish'ah B'Av* if they want to learn from *Tish'ah' B'Av*.[6] Following Ezekiel in part, the Rabbis thus come up with the following dictum: "All the commandments that are customary for mourning are customary for *Tish'ah B'Av*" (*Ta'anit* 30a). In order to determine these mourning practices, the Rabbis used a number of scriptural sources as prooftexts- including Ezekial 24.[7] From Ezekiel the Rabbis identify six mourning practices.[8] Four are derived (negatively) from instructions given to Ezekiel concerning mourning practices that he was *not* to observe: he was told to wear his regular garment, to wear sandals, to go uncovered, and to not eat "the bread of comforters" (24.17). He also was told to "moan softly" (or "silently": "*ha'onek dom*). From these two words enjoining silence upon Ezekiel, the Rabbis learned that he was commanded *to follow* the mourning practices of not greeting people (not saying "shalom" to them), and of not learning "words of Torah".[9] The dimensions of this prohibition on studying Torah are subject to some debate in the Talmud, and this particular prohibition bears closer scrutiny. We will see that whereas Ezekiel gives us insight into how *suffering* should be interpreted, the Talmudic debate draws our attention to the interpretation of suffering.

Interpreting Suffering

The Talmud says that on *Tish'ah B'Av*, just like during mourning, "it is forbidden to read in the Torah, *Nevi'im* [Prophets], *Ketuvim* [Writings], and to learn the Mishnah, Talmud, midrash, *halachot* [laws] or *aggadot* [stories], but it is permissible to read from a text that one is not used to reading, and to study a text that one is not used to studying (*Ta'anit* 30a). Rabbi Yehuda argues with this position on studying Torah, however; and his position is to become halachah (law). He says that "One may not even read from a text that one is not used to reading, nor study a text that one is not used to studying," and he continues (as did the earlier position) that "one may read from Job, lamentations, and the harsh things in Jeremiah; and the children are excused from their studies, for it is written: 'The precepts of the Lord are just, rejoicing the heart' [Psalm 19.9]". We see here in the Talmud that the act of interpretation itself must be considered in the interpretation of suffering. (That this was a major concern of the Rabbis can be illustrated by their refusal in this case, unlike in many others, to except the education of children from a prohibition.) Common to both positions is the idea that the act of study might take a person out of the spirit of the day. The former position excludes texts with which one is unfamiliar (either because the unfamiliarity is itself a source of pain for that person, or because the exertion of studying the text will prove painful).[10] whereas Rabbi Yehuda holds that the act of learning is inherently so pleasurable that learning must be restricted to texts that specifically discuss or portray suffering.[11] Only these portions are painful enough to compensate for the positive process of interpretation. From the Talmudic consensus we learn that the act of interpreting suffering is inherently problematic and perilous. The very act of interpretation undermines a person's comprehension of suffering. This teaching from the Talmud is quite pertinent today in academia, with the growth of the field known as Holocaust Studies. Many people studying the Holocaust have for some time been aware of the inherent tension in their field: In order to study the Holocaust and keep one's sanity, one has to circle around the horror; in circling around the horror one is not studying the Holocaust. The Talmud allows us now to add: In circling around the horror, scholarship may undercut Holocaust. The joy, honour, and prestige of scholarship accrue to Holocaust scholars just as they do to those engaged in other areas of study. Holocaust scholars could learn from Ezekiel that it is difficult to interpret suffering from a standpoint outside of suffering, and they could learn from the Talmud that the very act of interpreting undermines the interpretation of suffering. This is not to say that Holocaust scholars need to engage in ritualised suffering, or that attempts to study the Holocaust should be abandoned. It is to suggest that in order to produce good scholarship, Holocaust scholars need to articulate and reflect more upon the spirit behind their enquiry.

The Rituals of Tish'ah B'Av

If *Tish'ah B'Av* is a day given over to ritual suffering, it is appropriate to briefly review these rituals and then to ask how affective and effective is this day in allowing people to interpret suffering. *Tish'ah B'Av's* impact, however, should not be assessed in isolation, for it is the final and climactic moment of a whole period of ritualises mourning.[12] This period begins three weeks before *Tish'ah B'Av* with the fast of *Shiv'ah 'Asar Be Tamuz*, the seventeenth day of Tamuz (commemorating the breaching of the walls of Jerusalem). With the fast of the seventeenth of Tamuz, the Jewish people enter the period known as the "days between the fences" (*"bein ha'metzarim"*).[13]The rabbis speak of this three week period as days of affliction (*"metzarim"* shares the same root with *"tzara"* "affliction"). This is the bleakest period of the Jewish year: marriages are not performed, new clothing is not worn; people refrain from listening to music, from dancing, from haircutting (including shaving), from pleasure trips, and from situations of potential danger. As the three weeks progress, more stringencies for ritualised suffering are added. The first day of the month of Av begins a period known as "the nine days". During this time the consumption of meat or wine is prohibited (with the exception of the Sabbath and certain special "meals of mitzvah"). Clothes-washing is also forbidden, as is pleasure bathing. The week of *Tish'ah B'Av* is known as *"shavu'a she-chal bo"* ("the week in which it falls"). During this week people will be extra stringent upon themselves concerning the ritualised suffering practices of the nine days and of the three weeks. One can see, therefore, that by the time *Tish'ah B'Av* arrives, religiously observant Jews are already primed for an experience of heightened ritualised suffering. The more one has set the tone for *Tish'ah B'Av* during the preceding three weeks, the more *Tish'ah B'Av* will be affective and effective as ritualised suffering.

Tish'ah B'Av has two main moments: a dominant period of utter devastation and, towards the end of the day, a time of consolation (amidst the pain). Before the day begins a large (vegetarian) meal is eaten since, like *Yom Kippur* (the Day of

Atonement), *Tish'ah B'Av* is a twenty-five hour fast.[14] This is followed by a symbolic meal, typically of bread (sometimes dipped in ashes) and a hard-boiled egg.[15] Upon arriving at synagogue one notices some changes: People will sit on benches without cushions, or on the floor; and they will either go without shoes or wear shoes containing no leather. The covering of the ark in the synagogue has been removed, and lights are dimmed. Evening service is prayed in a subdued tone. And then the haunting melody of *Eichah* (Lamentations): "How?"[16] For those Jews who come to know the Hebrew Scriptures first as it is chanted in synagogue, the meaning of the text cannot be separated from the melody. This is certainly true for the plaintive rising and falling of the *Eichah* melody. The tune is so memorable that one hears it in one's mind in anticipation of the first verse read by the leader. The melody gives beautiful expression to the mournful feelings of the congregation. *Eichah* is not a narrative of what happened to the Jews and their Temples so much as it is a *lament* for what happened. It is a stupifying, shuddering "How?": "How lonely sits the city once great with people....(Lam.1.1). "*Eichah*" is not a question in search of historical- or even religious- answers so much as it is a question that serves to express the anguish of a bereaved people.

After the reading of *Eichah*, a small number of *kinnot* (lamentations) are recited to conclude the service. These are dirges, incorporating verses of *Eichah* into their text, and some are sung with the melody of *Eichah*.[17] Back at home, the observant will alter their usual sleep practices. This may mean sleeping without a pillow, or sleeping on the floor. "Some place a stone beneath their pillow or mattress in remembrance of the destruction" (Kitov 220). The synagogue service in the morning is the only weekday service of the year in which *tallit* (prayer shawl) and *tefillin* (phylacteries) are not worn. The synagogue still looks as it did the night before, and the congregants resume sitting on the floor or on cushionless seats. The Torah reading for the morning (Deut. 4.25-40) reminds the people that they will be punished if they disobey God's commandments, but emphasises the everlasting covenant and the rewards that will accrue for keeping the faith. The haftorah from Jeremiah (8.13-9.23) is bleak, with prophesies of doom for the sinful people: "The carcasses of men shall lie like dung upon the fields, like sheaves behind the reaper, with none to pick them up" (9.21). There follows a very long selection of 46 *kinnot*, and some people will recite lamentations all morning long. The final *kinnah*, "*Eli Tzion*" ("Wail, O Zion"), is sung in a powerful, assertive, affirmative tone. The melody is so wonderful that it does much to undercut the gloomy content of the *kinnah.*[18] "*Eli Tzion*" already anticipates the second phase of *Tish'ah B'Av*, one that is marked by some consolation.

Tish'ah B'Av and Job

When the congregation returns for the afternoon service, they find the synagogue looking like it normally does, and those sections and practices omitted from the morning service are reinstated (*tallit* and *tefillin*, for example, are donned). A special section of consolation, "*Nachem*, is added to the main prayer (the "*Amidah*"), beseeching God to "console the mourners of Zion and the mourners of Jerusalem and the city that is mournful, ruined, scorned, and desolate....."[19] The readings at this service are the same as on any other public fast day afternoon: from Exod. 32.11-14, 34.1-10, and from Isaiah 55.6-56.6. It is at this point in the day that one senses a lost opportunity for interpreting suffering. The readings here are certainly appropriate in that they reconnect this day to the rest of the year and take some tacit steps forwards, with the Torah's message of a second chance [symbolised by the giving of the second set of Tablets), and the haftorah's of an in-gathering of the exiled to the land of Israel. But there is also the opportunity here for some serious reflection on suffering- especially given the fact that this moment comes after 21 days of ritualised suffering and about 21 hours of heightened ritualised suffering. On *Tish'ah B'Av* we ask how suffering could have taken place but we don't ask why it occurred. We read the Book of Lamentations and ask the hauntingly powerful "*Eichah*", "How", but we never ask "Why"- in other words, we never read Job.

The Book of Job is the booking asking the "Why" question regarding suffering. The Jewish community needs to pay more attention to Job, especially after the Holocaust. It needs to ask "Why?" not because it will get any answers, but because questioning "Why?" is a crucial a Jewish response to suffering as is questioning "How?". Indeed, asking "Why?" might in itself constitute a pragmatic answer. I think we can see this in Ezekiel 24. Ezekiel's strange mourning practices are to act as a portent to the Jews; and how is this so? Because Ezekiel's behaviour brings the people to ask him about it. It engages them, and once they are engaged they are brought into dialogue; and learning, and perhaps repentance can then take place. Currently, though Job is one of the few works that are permitted to be studied on *Tish'ah B'Av*, the book receives no public reading and in practice just about no study on *Tish'ah B'Av*- or on any other day. I suggest that on *Tish'ah B'Av* afternoon the Jewish people is ready to ask "Why?". At the service marking a slight easing to the mourning of the day, the question of why suffering occurs can be humbly broached. This, of course, is not to replace "How", "*Eichah*". The bemoaning of what happened, the "How?" *should* take precedence. We first need to absorb all that happened. Yet as the day wanes, as we begin to think about the close of the *Tish'ah B'Av* experience, it is good to think "Why?".[20] Reading and studying Job might yield some fruitful results, challenging results. I will end here by suggesting one of these.

It may very well be the case that Job's wife needs to be held up as a theological model (and perhaps her words may also resurrect the voice of Ezekiel's wife, who, allowed a change to speak, might have questioned the methods God uses to get his point across). Job's wife, unnamed and in the background as a breeder for her husband's total of twenty children, says to Job: "You still keep your integrity! Blaspheme God and die!" (2.9). I have always thought that this was pretty good advice for a man who has just had all ten of his children die, whose finances are in ruins, and who is afflicted with an excruciatingly painful skin condition. It might even be the case that Job accepts this advice, for in the ensuing chapters he proclaims his innocence and does question God. Indeed, two classic Jewish commentators imply that it is Job's wife's suggestion that gets Job started on the road of "sinful" questioning. While Job apparently rejects his wife's advice (saying: "You talk as any shameless women night talk! Should we accept only good from God and not accept evil?"), both Rashi and Ibn Ezra point out that the text would have us believe otherwise. They draw our attention to the significance of the narrative comment after the rejection: "*be-chol zot lo chata iyov be-sfatav*", "For all that, Job said nothing sinful" (2.10). Noticing that the last word of the verse, "*be-sfatav*" ("with his lips"), is seemingly redundant, Rashi says that it implies that Job had *already* sinned in his heart. Ibn Ezra states that this word signals to the reader that Job will *eventually* sin with his lips and "utter words because of his great suffering". The question that Job's wife prompts Job to ask ("Should we accept only good from God and not accept evil?"), the question that Job thought to use to stifle his wife, becomes an open question in the book. His wife's position, formulated in his own words, begins to seem less "shameless" to Job than he thought. And though Rashi, Ibn Ezra, and the narrator apparently would say that Job's "sin" originates in this question, perhaps the book undercuts this reading by suggesting that given the ending, Job's wife was right to get her husband thinking and questioning. After all, at the end of the book, God rewards Job and scolds the three men who put forth a traditional position on suffering (they suggest that somehow the sufferer Job was at fault). Questioning, arguing- even blaspheming- may, the book suggests, be a more pious reaction than mute submission. We've seen this before in the bible, this kind of brazen *chutzpah*: with Abraham arguing with God over Sodom (Ge. 18.20-33), and with Moses persuading God not to destroy the Israelites (Num. 14.11-25). If one has a relationship with God and God is in some way responsible for one's suffering, then, as Job's wife may be suggesting, blasphemy is warranted precisely out of a commitment to the integrity of that covenantal relationship. I am reminded here of Elie Wiesel's famous story of God being put on trial by a group of Jewish prisoners in a Nazi concentration camp. God is found to be guilty. This is blasphemy, isn't it, to say that God is guilty? But then the very same group that conducted the trial goes to pray. God may be guilty, but the covenant may still hold and prayer may still be appropriate. An annual reading of at least a portion of the Book of Job could help the Jewish community with issues such as these. *Tish'ah B'Av*, with its system of ritualized suffering, is the best day for this reading since it provides Jews with a ritual framework from where they can interpret suffering- and ask why it occurs. And, in turn, a public reading from the book of Job would make it clear to all that *Tish'ah B'Av* is a ritual journey into suffering and not just a commemoration of two specific times of great suffering (during the destruction of the Temples). After all, that midrash on Numbers 14 can be read not just as saying that *Tish'ah B'Av* is a day on which something was to happen to warrant generations of crying, but as saying that on *Tish'ah B'Av* crying is obligatory for the generations- for the generations of human beings who suffered and for the generations of human beings who continue to suffer.

NOTES

1. The midrash is built upon the last two words of the verse: "ba-laylah ha-hu" ("that night"). If we remember that for the Rabbis, scripture is Torah (Teaching), the question that the midrash addresses becomes clear: What does this verse want to teach us by going out of its way to specify that the crying took place "that night"?

2. How *Tish'ah B'Av* is observed will vary according to the different branches of Judaism and from community to community. There are many different ways to use the sources I examine for situating *Tish'ah B'Av* as ritualised suffering.

3. This date is indicated because we know that Ezekiel dates his oracles from Jehoiachin's coronation in 598 BCE, and 24.1 reads: "In the ninth year, on the tenth day of the tenth month, the word of the Lord came to me." For a brief scholarly review of Ezekiel, see Lawrence Boadt, *Reading the Old Testament: An Introduction* (Mahwah: Paulist Press, 1984): 386-398.

4. The earlier part of the chapter is an allegory concerning the people's inability to have their iniquity purged from them. Ezekiel is instructed to cook a stew of meat until it is burnt away, since the time of forgiveness is past and the time of destruction is at hand.

5. I use the Jewish Publication Society's *Tanakh: The Holy Scriptures* (Philadelphia: JPS, 1985) for all my biblical translations in this work. Here I also follow their reading- which positions verse 24 after verse 21 for clarity.

6. The Talmud (in *Ta'anit* 30b) formulates this religious message in a poetic way when it declares: "All who mourn for Jerusalem will be privileged to see it in its happiness [*be-simchatah*, in its rebuilt glory], and whoever does not mourn for Jerusalem will not see it in its happiness." Isaiah 66.10 is given as prooftext: "Rejoice with Jerusalem and be glad for her, All you who love her! Join in her jubilation, All you who mourned over her."

7. The fullest Talmudic discussion of mourning practices can be found in *Moed Katan*, *"Alu Megalchin"* (chapter 3; 13b ff.).

8. Besides these practices derived from Ezekiel 24, there are other mourning prohibitions operative on *Tish'ah B'Av* such as those on washing, on anointing with oil, and on sexual relations; and there are two special prohibitions (that are not operative for mourners) forbidding the consumption of food and drink.

9. The apparent inconsistency of formulating mourning customs by *following* Ezekiel's example in two cases while using his behaviour as a negative example in four other practices was not lost upon classic Talmudic commentators. One solution was to show that the verse itself makes a distinction between the two practices Ezekiel is to share with other mourners and the four he is not- since these four are introduced with the words "observe no mourning for the dead" (24.17). Ezekiel was allowed to express mourning for his wife in the two practices indicated by "moan softly" because these were more private practices and difficult to detect. (For the four practices that would be apparent to all, he was required to abstain and act as a "portent"). Another solution to the problem was to say that this whole discussion falls in the realm of *"asmachta"* ("support"). That is, the Rabbis really were not deriving customs from Ezekiel; they were *already* relying upon traditional customs and sought prooftexts to ground these practices in Holy Scripture. See *Talmud Bavli: Masechet Moed Katan*, ed. and trans. Adin Steinsaltz, vol.12 (Jerusalem: Israel Institute for Talmudic Publications, 1984) 68n. (15a).

10. See *Talmud Bavli: Masechet Ta'anit*, ed. and trans. Adin Steinsaltz, vol.11 (Jerusalem: Israel Institute for Talmudic Publications, 1989) 131n. (30a).

11. In addition to the texts mentioned here in the Talmud, the only other Torah to be studied by mourners and on *Tish'ah B'Av* would be the third chapter from *Moed Katan* (cited above, and the laws of mourning.

12. For a review of the relevant laws and traditions pertaining to this period see Eliyahu Kitov, *The Book of Our Heritage: The Jewish Year and Its Days of Significance*, trans. Nathan Bulman, 3 vols. (Jerusalem: Feldheim, 1978) 3:193-207 [for Tamuz]; and 3:211-315 [for Av].

13. This name comes from Lamentations 1,3: "All her [Judah's] pursuers overtook her in the narrow places *(bein ha-metzarim)*."

14. In practice, the prohibitions on *Tish'ah B'Av* are almost identical with those of Yom Kippur. The difference is that Yom Kippur has the status of a *Yom Tov (holiday)* and no work is permitted. On *Tish'ah B'Av*, though work is permitted, one is encouraged to keep one's focus on the spirit of the day. There are also traditions saying that the ninth of Av used to be a festive day and that when the Messiah (who will be born on *Tish'ah B'Av*) comes, *Tish'ah B'Av* will revert back to its original Holiday status.

15. One of the symbolisms behind eating the egg will interest us here. Besides symbolising a cosmic order to the universe (eggs, like planets and their orbits, are elliptical) the egg has no opening- no mouth. Symbolically, mourners too are mouth-less, since (as we saw from Ezekiel and the Talmud) they cannot greet people or study most of the Torah.

16. Though the Jewish Publication Society translates *"Eichah"* as "Alas", translating it as "how" is perfectly acceptable since *"eichah"* builds directly upon the Hebrew word for "how": *"eich"*. It is translated this way in *The Jerusalem Bible* (Jerusalem: Koren, 1980). Significantly, Rabbi Moses Isserles (the Rama) states that the leader should bring out the "How?" by emphasising the word *"eichah"* each of the several times it comes up in the book (qtd. in Kitov 222).

17. The melody to *Eichah* is used on a number of occasions to remind the congregation of the loss of the Temples. For example, the tune is used for Deut. 1.9 (part of the Torah reading of Deut.1.1-3.22 during the Sabbath preceding *Tish'ah B'Av*): "How [eichah] can I bear unaided the trouble of you, and the burden, and the bickering". Much of the haftorah for this Sabbath (Isaiah 1.1-27) is also read with the *Eichah* melody. And on Purim, the phrase *"ve-calim micalim shonim"* ("beakers of varied design", Esther 1.7) is sung with the *Eichah* tune to signal to the listener that the vessels described were taken from the looted (First) Temple.

18. In the Friday night service preceding the week of *Tish'ah Av* the prayer *"Lechah Dodi"* ("Come My Beloved") is often sung to the tune of *"Eli Tzion"*. The tune expresses the sense that though there will be a day of sharp mourning ahead (and though there have been many days of mourning in the past), the Jewish people lives and will live on.

19. See *The Complete Tish'ah B'Av Service, Nusach* [tradition of] *Ashkenaz*, eds. Avrohom Chaim Feuer and Avie Gold (Brooklyn: Mesorah, 1991] 433.

20. What I am describing here reflects a similar pattern to the way I teach the Holocaust. First there is a confrontation with the horror of the Holocaust, and then there is *The Reawakening*. (This is the title of Primo Levi's book describing his journey home from Auschwitz after the war). For the horror, one responds with a dumbfounded "How?". For the reawakening, it becomes necessary to ask "Why?"- politically, historically, economically, theologically. See Primo Levi *The Reawakening*, 1965, trans. Stuart Woolf (New Work: Macmillan, 1987).

Chapter V

THE CHARACTER OF APOPHATIC KNOWLEDGE IN MAIMONIDES' GUIDE

José Faur

The Dialectics of Apophatic Knowledge

Apophaticism, underscoring the limits of human understanding and the absolute transcendence of God, is the master-key to Maimonides' (1135-1204) intellectual apparatus. It is a different class of knowledge, superior to common rationality and inferior to prophecy. This knowledge is grounded on a special kind of dialectics generated by "positive attributes/negative attributes". As will be seen in what follows, an adequate conception of apophaticism is essential if we are to come to grips with Maimonides' negative theology. There are three aspects to his theology. First, there are linguistic considerations preventing the application of positive attributes or any kind of cataphatic knowledge to God.[1] Secondly, epistemologically, human intelligence is limited and there are subjects transcending human understanding.[2] Finally, ontologically, the notion of positive attributes, contradicts the doctrine of absolute monotheism[3] Since the biblical doctrine of creation posits that there is no ontological relationship between God and His creatures[4] all attributes referring to God Himself, including those positing His existence, being, and omniscience, must be interpreted negatively. In the words of Maimonides:

> Absolutely, there is no likeness between Him and his creatures in anything. His existence is not like their existence, His life is not like

the life of those who live, and His knowledge is not like the knowledge of those who know.[5]

Knowledge of God is attained *via negativa*. Concerning the apophatic knowledge resulting from such a methodology, Maimonides raised a fundamental question:

> One may ask: Since there are no means by which His true essence could be comprehended, and proofs can only demonstrate that He exists,[6] and as it was demonstrated, positive attributes [of God] are impossible, in which way can there be any distinction among those who comprehend Him? Since according to this [it would appear that], whatever our Teacher Moses and Solomon comprehended is that which a common student had comprehended.[7]

Epistemologically, positive attributes are a hindrance to our knowledge of God. Maimonides characterised those necessitating a positive attribute to God, such as corporeality or any other attribute which is demonstrably inapplicable to God, as "blind".[8] Therefore, the more attributes are negated of God, the nearer one comes to Him. Maimonides made the essential point that in the same fashion that positive attributes increase our knowledge of an object, the negation of positive attributes increases our knowledge of God:

> Because the more one increases the positive description of an object, the more definite the described (object) becomes, and the describer (subject) comes closer to comprehend its true essence. In the same fashion, the more [positive attributes] that you negate of Him, blessed by He, the closer you are in comprehension, and the closer you are to Him than one who does not negate [from Him the attribute] which was demonstrated (*tubarhan*) to you its negation.[9]

This means that apophatic knowledge is not merely the rejection of a positive attribute, or the correction of a mistaken opinion. To be significant, apophasis must maintain a dialectical relationship with the positive attribute that it negates. It is a dynamic process: the very process of negating a positive attribute constitutes and defines apophasis. This negation cannot be accomplished either by removing a contradiction or amending a mistake, and accepting the 'right' view on the basis of faith. Rather, it requires demonstration on the basis of *burhan* (plural *burahin*)- 'proof' based on the principle of contradiction- the impossibility to apply such an attribute to God. According, there are two moments to the negation of positive attributes. Initially, there is negation of a positive attribute without a positive proof (*burhan*). At this level, no apophatic knowledge is realised, and doubt will linger in the mind of the believer. The second movement involves a positive proof (*burhan*) demonstrating why such a positive attribute cannot apply to God. It is only at that level that apophatic knowledge is realised. Referring to an individual attaining only the first level, as someone who is "intellectually ineffectual", Maimonides distinguished between people to whom it was not "demonstrated" (*turbarhan*) the cancellation of a positive attribute, and consequently in doubt, and people "who know with a proof (*bi-al-burhan*) that it is impossible to apply to Him such a subject".[10] To attain this second level, arduous work may be necessary:

> Therefore, a man would occasionally need to toil a few years in the understanding of certain science and the demonstration (*tubarhan*) of its foundations, until he is certain; the sole result of such knowledge would be to negate from God certain subject which was demonstrated (*bi-' al-burhan*) that it is impossible to apply to Him.[11]

It is only through apophatic knowledge, based on demonstrable proofs (*burahin*), that one draws closer to God.[12] Those attaining apophatic knowledge have attained *kamala*, human 'perfection', and are designated by the code-term *kamilun* 'perfects'.[13] They are "men of perfection" (*al-kamalun*) and worthy of knowing the secrets of the Prophetic writings".[14] This type of perfection is capable of gradation. As Maimonides puts it:

> It has thus been explained to you that whenever it has been proven (*tubarhan*) to you the negation of something which is not in Him, you are more perfect (*'akmal*), and whenever you have necessitated something additional to Him, you are being confused and have furthered yourself away from knowing His true [essence]. It is in this fashion that one must come to His comprehension, through scrutiny and investigation, until the impossibility of applying to Him whatever is impossible to apply to Him, is known. Without ascribing to Him something that adds to his essence.[15]

Since apophasis results in a definite knowledge of God, the more attributes are negated of Him the better understanding of His essence.[16] Hence the excellence of the educated conception of God over the notions of "the common student".[17]

Apophasis and Paradox

Structurally, apophasis or negative knowledge, involves a double paradox, whereby "knowledge/non-knowledge" give rise to "praise/silence".

There are two fundamental aspects to apophasis. First, structurally, apophaticism involves an essential paradox. On the one hand, it is the only means by which humankind may achieve perfection and true knowledge of God. On the other hand, it is only upon fully developing human intellectual abilities, and realising their inability to comprehend God, that humans fulfil their full potential. Therefore apophatic knowledge of God is *not* to understand Him in a double sense: we understand Him precisely upon realising that He cannot be understood; when we think that we understand Him then we really do not understand Him. Maimonides writes:

> And when everyone realised (*sha'ara*) that there is no mean to reach what we can potentially perceive but negatively, and negation does not inform anything at all about the truth of the subject from which the thing that was negated was negated, it is transparent to all humans, past and future, that God blessed be He cannot be comprehended by the minds, and that nobody can comprehend who is He but He, and that to comprehend Him is the inability to fully comprehend Him.[18]

Secondly, and as a consequence of the first, the ultimate perception reached through apophaticism defies linguistic expression and cannot be communicated. Absolute silence, in the sense of total absence of articulated speech and thought, is essential to the apophatic experience.[19] This, too, involves an essential paradox: silence is praise and praise is silence. Maimonides writes:

> And all the philosophers shall say (*yaqulun*): "We were illuminated by His Splendor but (He) is hidden from us by the might of His lucidity, just like the sun is hidden from the sight which is weak to perceive it."[20] This was extensively elaborated [by others] and needs not to be repeated here. The foremost of what was said on this topic is what was said in *Psalms* (65:2): "*Lekha Dumya Tehilla*". Translation: To You silence is praise. This is a very profound statement on this matter. Because whatever we intend to say to exalt and praise Him would be found faulty when applied to Him, feeling somehow that it is wanting. Silence is therefore fundamental, and brevity is

proportional to the understanding of the minds. As it was prescribed by those who are perfect (*'al-kamilun*) (Ps. 4:5), "Speak up in your hearts upon your beds, and be silent. Selah".[21]

Because of its paradoxical structure expressed in the dialectics "knowledge ->non-knowledge", and its concomitant "praise->silence", apophatic knowledge may be compared to a succession of flashes of light in the darkness. Referring to this type of knowledge, Maimonides wrote: "Sometimes the truth shines upon us, and we suppose it to be [as clear as] in daylight, and behold it is then concealed by body and habits!"[22] Maimonides compared this type of truth "to the flame of the spinning sword" guarding the entrance of Eden (Gen.3:24) that "shines and then is concealed".[23] Accordingly, apophatic knowledge cannot be communicated:

> Know that when one of the man of perfection (*'al-kamlin*) in accordance to the level of his perfection (*kamalhu*) wishes to express something of what he had understood about these secrets, either orally or in writing, he cannot explain- even the measure of what he comprehended- thoroughly and orderly as it is done in the other sciences commonly studied. But he would experience when teaching others the same situation in which he found himself when he learned it. Namely, that the subject will surface and emit, and then be concealed; as if the nature of this subject would remain unchanged, whether [comprehending] of it a little or much.[24]

This is why, all apophatic knowledge is esoteric.[25] The entire structure of the *Guide* rests on this principle.

Perplexity and Subjectivity

Maimonides begins the *Guide* with an epistle addressed to a student. In the epistle, Maimonides narrates the circumstances bringing to him a student who wanted to know the "secrets of the Prophetic writings". We are told about his educational and intellectual background, his staying and eventual departure, and how his parting prompted Maimonides to write the *Guide*. it ends with a dedicatory note stating that [a] his absence induced him "to fashion (*li-wada'a*) this work which I had fashioned (*wada'taha*) for you and those who are like you, although are few"; [b] and that he had "made" the *Guide* into "scattered *(mantura)* chapters, and all that was written of it, it would reach you one by one wherever you are, and you (be in) peace".

There are several problems with this epistle. It seems anecdotal and out of character with the *Guide*. The few points of philosophical interest concerning the educational intellectual background of the student, serving to identify the readership for which the *Guide* was intended, were spelled out by Maimonides in the Introduction.[26] In particular, the circumstances prompting Maimonides to write the *Guide* appear to be irrelevant. What could the philosophical significance be that Maimonides had written the *Guide* after his disciple had left? Or that instead of a complete volume he would be receiving the *Guide* in instalments.

As mentioned before, apophatic knowledge cannot be communicated. This affects the methodology and aims underlying the relationship teacher-student. In other sciences and disciplines, there must be maintained a hierarchical relationship between teacher and student. Knowledge is transmitted vertically. The student recognises the *authority* of the teacher. The teacher 'transmits' *(moser)* and the student 'accepts' *(meqabbel)* authoritative knowledge. Indeed, the vertical process 'passing on->accepting' *(mesira->qabbala)* is essential to the transmission and authority of the Oral Law.[27] This process, however, can never be applied to esoteric knowledge. Since esoteric knowledge cannot be transmitted hierarchically, it cannot be the subject of '*qabbala*', authoritative acceptance.[28] Rather, it demands absolute horizontality between the transmitor and the recipient. The Rabbis had determined that the teacher "surrenders" *(mosrin)* to the student only "the heads of chapters"- that is, the basic axioms, not the actual knowledge to be inferred from them- and then the student "must understand in his own mind".[29] Thus, hierarchical transmission of esoteric knowledge is not only impossible, it is forbidden to attempt- more precisely, to pretend.[30] Therefore, Maimonides writes, "don't ask of me here for more than the heads of chapters".[31] Upon receiving these "heads of chapters", the student must approach the subject independently of his teacher.[32] The task of the teacher is to goad the student to the cross-road; facing "perplexity" *(haira)*, a crisis of choice, the student is "perplexed" *(ha'iran)* and must make his own decision.[33] This knowledge is never hierarchically transmitted; rather, it is "transferred"- that is horizontally- "from one bosom to the other".[34]

It is only upon breaking the umbilical cord with the teacher and deciding to face 'perplexity' on his own, that the student could be exposed to the technique leading to apophatic knowledge and esoteric lore. It is worth observing that in the dedicatory note Maimonides did not refer to the writing of the *Guide* with the more common term '*allafa* ('to write', 'to compose'), and *ta'alif* ('composition of a book'),[35] but with *wada'a* ('to fashion', 'to author'). Significantly, this term also means 'to give birth'. Therefore, the absence of the student was not only a stimulus, but rather a condition *sine qua non*, for producing the *Guide*.

We can now approach the second point, that the *Guide* had been "made" into "scattered (*mantura*) chapters", that "would reach you one by one wherever you are". As Maimonides had explained, the "heads of chapters" or basic axioms contained in the *Guide* are neither "in order nor in succession, but mingled and combined" with other matters requiring explanation.[36] Maimonides is here assuring his student, thereby the attentive reader, that eventually, after a period of maturation and autonomous thinking, the subtextual order of the *Guide* will "reach" him "one by one" regardless of time and place. Note that Maimonides did not state that the chapters will be "sent" to the student one by one, but, rather, that they will "reach" him one by one, that is, in due course.

There are other aspects of the term *mantura* ('scattered') essential for a proper understanding of the *Guide*. The root of this term is *natara*, which also means 'to write in prose'; the form *natr* not only means 'prose', but 'style'. Accordingly, the 'scattering' of the material concerns the literary style and structure of the *Guide*. Maimonides could have chosen one of two styles. He could have chosen an expository style, without a dialogue, like the philosophical work of Se'adya Gaon (882-942), or a dialogic form in which he converses with a partner, like the philosophical works of Solomon ibn Gabirol (ca. 1020-ca. 1057) and Judah ha-Levi (ca. 1075-1141). Instead, Maimonides, developed a special type of expository technique. At the surface the *Guide* contains no dialogues. However, at the subtextual level there is a sustained dialogue initiated- not by Maimonides- but by a student in search of "the secrets of the Prophetic writings" - a student representing the reader for whom the *Guide* was written. Maimonides, a teacher limited by the constrains of the law and the nature of the subject,[37] is a partner responding to the student/reader. The principal task of the teacher is to develop a technique of indirect communication and guide the student/reader towards *ḥaira* ('perplexity'). This technique is closely related to another aspect of *naṯara*. The form *naṯri* means both 'prosaic' and 'small fragment'. Maimonides' technique consists in the *naṯr* ('scattering') of *nuṯar* ('small tiny fragments'). This leads directly to the concept of parergon, or ornamentation of the text.[38] In the case of the *Guide* the function of the parergon is exactly the opposite of that described by Kant. Rather than to expose and enhance the object that it contains, the function of the parergon in the *Guide* is to conceal the tiny fragments containing the "heads of chapters". In turn, because these fragments are scattered in a (apparently) disorderly fashion, they, too, function as the parergon of the parergon: it would be the task of the student/reader to determine what is ornamental and what is substantive in the *Guide*; or: what is the light and what is the darkness concealing the light. Only that student/reader worthy of being initiated into the "secrets of the Prophetic writings" would make the right choices.

An effect of this technique is that the apophatic experience of the student/reader will be absolutely subjective. The teacher is not an intermediary shaping, affecting, and controlling the perception of the student/reader. His task is only to guide, not in an 'authoritative', 'objective' fashion, but as a *dalala* (a 'sing post') pointing out externally to the student/reader till he reaches a state of *ḥaira* ('perplexity'). The (*ḥa'iran*) 'perplexed' must then face a crisis of pure choice, and therefore of pure subjectivity. Hence the two terms making up the title of the *Guide (Dalalat) of the Perplexed ('al-Ha'irin).*[39] It would then be up to the student/reader to establish (or not to establish) a direct relationship with God, and of determining (or not determining) the experience 'knowledge->non-knowledge', 'praise->silence'.

73

NOTES

1. See my *Golden Doves with Silver Dots: Semiotics and Textuality in Rabbinic Tradition* (Bloomington: Indiana University Press, 1986), pp.70-83.

2. See Maimonides *Guide for the Perplexed* (henceforth: *Guide*) I, 31-32. All references and pagination refer to the Arabic original, *Dalalat al-Hairin*, ed. Issachar Joel (Jerusalem: J. Junovitch, 5691 [1930/31]). The translations are mine. References are to section, chapter, page and line of the Arabic original.

3. Ibid., I, 51.

4. See *Golden Doves*. pp. 79. 175 note 47.

5. *Guide* I, 35, p. 54 (11. 8-10).

6. But nothing more, see ibid. 58.

7. *Guide* I, 59, pp. 93 (1.29)-94 (1.3).

8. Ibid., p.94 (1.13). Cf. ibid., "Introduction", p.4 (11. 8-12).

9. Ibid., p.94 (11. 5-8).

10. Ibid., (11. 4-13).

11. Ibid., 59, p.94 (11. 8-11).

12. See ibid., (11. 8-13).

13. This was one of the quality of the famous disciple to whom he dedicated the *Guide*, see ibid., "Introductory Epistle", p.1 (11. 6-7), and ibid., the "Introduction", pp.4 (1.12), 5 (1.2), 6 (1.1).

14. For a definition of such individuals, see ibid., "Introductory Epistle", p.1, specially 11. 14-15; "Introduction", p.4 (11. 7-8).

15. Ibid., 59, p.94 (11. 23-27).

16. See ibid., p.94 (11. 5-8), quoted above note 7.

17. See ibid., Introduction, p.4 (11. 7-8).

18. *Guide* I, 59, p.95 (11. 1-5).

19. Concerning the function of silence in Jewish mystical thought, see *Golden Doves*, pp. 116-117.

20. This statement was misunderstood by commentators and translators because they took the form *yaqulun* as a perfect ('said'), when in fact in the present continuum ('they say'). Obviously, Maimonides could not possibly have written that actually *all* philosophers have *made* such a statement. What Maimonides is clearly saying, and somehow had escaped the grasp of translators and commentators, is that all those who are (*genuine*) philosophers, i.e., who have attained apophatic knowledge, do acknowledge the above statement. Acknowledgement of the statement serves as an indicator of who really is a "(genuine) philosopher".

21. *Guide* I, 59, p.95 (11. 5-13).

22. Ibid., Introduction, p.3 (11. 25-26).

23. Ibid., (11. 6-7). Maimonide's point becomes clear upon realising that the Hebrew term *mithappekhet* commonly translated "revolving", "spinning", stems from *hafakh* "to turn around", "to change and become the opposite", see Ex.14:5. Accordingly, rather than "the spinning sword", the exact translation is "the sword which becomes its opposite".

24. Ibid., p.4 (11. 12-17).

25. Although not necessarily the reverse.

26. See p.6 (11. 10-12); and I, 35.

27. On the precise meaning and function of these terms, see *Golden Doves*, pp.14, 123-124.

28. This is another instance confirming the view that Medieval Kabbalah is the effect of intellectual assimilation and essentially alien to Rabbinic Judaism. See my "Two Models of Jewish Spirituality", *Shofar* 10 (1992), 5-46. I have further developed this theme in a forthcoming article, "A Crisis of Categories: Kabbalah and the Rise of Apostasy in Spain", ed. Moshe Lazar, *The Jews of Spain and the Expulsion of 1492* (Los Angeles: University of Southern California).

29. Ḥagiga 13a. For an analysis of this passage, see *Golden Doves*, p.126.

30. See ibid., Introduction, p.3 (11. 2-7); III, Introduction, p.297 (11. 5-17).

31. *Guide*, Introduction, p.3 (1.11).

32. Hence the term *derasha* ('exposition') employed in this context, see Ḥagiga 15b and *Golden Doves*, p.126. Only a *bakham* ('sage')- not a student- is authorised to make *derasha*, see *Golden Doves*, p.xviii.

33. See *Golden Doves*, pp.75-76.

34. *Guide*, III, Introduction p.297 (1.19).

35. See ibid., p.298 (1.6).

36. Ibid., Introduction, p.3 (11. 12-14).

37. See above note 29.

38. On this fundamental concept, see our discussion in *Golden Doves*, pp.xxvii-xxviii, 216.

39. On this fundamental concept, and the precise sense of *dalala*, see *Golden Doves*, pp.74-76.

Chapter VI

GOD AND THE HOLOCAUST
Dan Cohn-Sherbok

Throughout their long history suffering has been the hallmark of the Jewish people. Driven from their homeland, buffeted from country to country and plagued by persecutions, Jews have been rejected, despised and led as a lamb to the slaughter. The Holocaust is the most recent chapter in this tragic record of events. The Third Reich's system of murder squads, concentration camps and killing centres eliminated nearly 6 million Jews; though Jewish communities had previously been decimated, such large scale devastation profoundly affected the Jewish religious consciousness. For many Jews it has seemed impossible to reconcile the concept of a loving, compassionate and merciful God with the terrible events of the Nazi regime.

Theology of Protest

Prominent among modern Jewish writers who have wrestled with the theological implications of the Holocaust is the novelist Elie Wiesel. At the concentration camp Birkenau, Wiesel came close to death as he marched toward a pit of flaming bodies only to stop a few feet from the edge. 'Never shall I forget those flames which consumed my faith forever',[1] he wrote. For Wiesel the Holocaust is inexplicable with God, but also it cannot be understood without Him. Auschwitz made it impossible for Wiesel to trust God's goodness, but it also made questions about God more important. In this regard Wiesel has been heard to remark: 'If I told you I believed in God, I would be lying'; if I told you I did not believe in God, I would be lying'.[2] Wiesel is thus at odds with God because the only way he can be for God after Auschwitz is by being against Him - to embrace God without protest would be to vindicate Him and legitimize evil.

This stance is eloquently portrayed in Wiesel's play, *The Trial of God* which is set in the village of Shamgorod during the season of Purim. Three Jewish actors have lost their way and arrive at the village which they discover is not the place for joyous celebration since it was devastated by a pogrom two years before. Only two Jews survived: Berish the innkeeper who escaped and his daughter who was abused on her wedding night and has now lost touch with the world. In the area of Shamgorod anti-Semitic hatred has flared up once again and a new pogrom appears imminent. The Festival of Purim calls for a play which will enact the trial of God. Yet there is a difficulty. None of the actors wants to speak up for God. Unnoticed however a stranger whose name is Sam enters the inn and volunteers to act as a defence attorney for God. It appears that Berish's Housekeeper Maria has seen this person before and she cautions Berish to have nothing to do with him. But despite this warning the play commences.

Berish begins his persecution by contending that God could use his power to save the victims, but He does not. 'So', he asks, 'on whose side is He? Could the killer kill without His blessing - without His complicity?'[3] Berish has no sympathy for the defendant: 'If I am given the choice of feeling sorry for Him or for human beings, I choose the latter anytime. He is big enough, strong enough to take care of Himself; man is not'.[4] In response Sam answers every accusation and urges that emotion should not take the place of evidence. The actors who have formed the court are impressed and inquire who Sam is. As the play concludes, a violent mob approaches the inn. Realising the end is near, the Jewish actors elect to die wearing their Purim masks. Sam puts a mask on as well, and Maria's premonition is confirmed - the mask he wears is that of Samael which signifies Satan. As a final candle is extinguished, the inn door opens to the sound of murderous tumult including Satan's laughter.

Though this play is not directly about the Holocaust since it is set three centuries previously, it does touch on the central theological dilemma posed by the death camps. As Wiesel explains in the foreword to the play and elsewhere, he witnessed a trial of God at Auschwitz where three rabbis who conducted the proceedings found God guilty and then participated in the daily prayer. The reason they performed this seemingly inconsistent act is related to a story Wiesel tells about a Spanish Jewish family that had been expelled from Spain.[5] Finding no refuge from continual persecution, the father who was the last to survive prayed:

> Master of the Universe, I know what you want - I understand what you are doing. You want despair to overwhelm me. You want me to cease invoking your name to glorify and sanctify it. Well, I tell you! No., no - a thousand times no! You shall not succeed! In spite of me and in spite of you, I shall shout the Kaddish, which is a song of faith, for You and against You. The song you shall not still, God of Israel.[6]

In stating his case for and against God, Wiesel emphasises that there was no need for God to allow the Holocaust to occur - it was an event that produced only death and destruction. Yet Wiesel asserts to be Jewish is 'never to give up - never to yield to despair'.[7] It is in this spirit that Wiesel conducts his dispute with God. As a survivor of the horrors of the death camps, Wiesel refuses to let God go. His struggles serve as a testimony that the religious quest was not incinerated in the gas chambers of the Nazi period.

Although Wiesel's literary works dealing with the Holocaust are not intended to provide a systematic theological response to the death camps, he does struggle with central religious questions. As we have seen, his experiences did not lead him to atheism, yet he repeatedly casts doubts on the traditional Jewish understanding of God. Unfortunately, in these reflections Wiesel does not clarify what position he adopts; his statement that he would be lying if he claimed both to believe in God and not to believe in Him simply highlights his own confusion. Thus for those who are anxious to find a solution to the theological dilemmas posed by the Holocaust, Wiesel's protest against God simply reinforces their religious perplexity and underscores the urgency of discovering a theodicy in which God's silence during World War II can be understood.

A Non-Theistic Response

Unlike Wiesel some Jewish thinkers have found it impossible to sustain a belief in the traditional understanding of God after the Holocaust. According to Richard Rubenstein - the most eloquent spokesman for this viewpoint - Auschwitz is the utter and decisive refutation of the traditional affirmation of a providential God who acts in history and watches over the Jewish people whom he has chosen from all nations. In *After Auschwitz* published in 1966, he writes:

> How can Jews believe in an omnipotent, beneficent God after Auschwitz? Traditional Jewish theology maintains that God is the ultimate, omnipotent actor in historical drama. It has interpreted every major catastrophe in Jewish history as God's punishment of a sinful Israel. I fail to see how this position can be maintained without regarding Hitler and the SS as instruments of God's will ... To see any purpose in the death camps, the traditional believer is forced to regard the most demonic, anti-human explosion of all history as a meaningful expression of God's purposes.[8]

In this study Rubenstein insists that the Auschwitz experience has resulted in a rejection of the traditional theology of history which must be replaced by a positive affirmation of the value of human life in and for itself without any special theological relationship. Joy and fulfilment are to be sought in this life, rather than in a mystical future or eschaton. Thus he maintains that we should attempt to establish contact with those powers of life and death which engendered the ancient Canaanites' feelings about Baal, Astarte and Anith. This would not mean literally a return to the actual worship of these deities, but simply that earth's fruitfulness, its vicissitudes and its engendering power will once again become the central spiritual realities of Jewish life. According to Rubenstein God is the ultimate nothing, and it is to this Divine source that man and the world are ultimately to return. There is no hope of salvation for mankind; man's ultimate destiny is to be returned to Divine nothingness. In this context Auschwitz fits into the archaic religious consciousness and observance of the universal cycle of death and rebirth. The Nazi slaughter of European Jewry was followed by the rebirth of the Jewish people in the land of Israel.

Today Rubenstein sees his position as akin to mystical religion. In a recent investigation of the origins of the Holocaust and its consequences on Jewish thought,[9] he notes that his loss of faith and the events of the Second World War caused him to have a bleak view of the world. But at present he would be more apt to adopt an optimistic stance. Yet what has remained the same is his insistence that the traditional conception of God needs to be rejected. Further he asserts that the Jews are not God's Divinely chosen people; they are a people like any other, whose religion was influenced by cultural and historical events. Some of Rubenstein's critics have asked whether anyone who accepts his view has any reason to remain Jewish since the Jewish heritage is infused with the belief that the Jews are under obligation to observe Divinely ordained commandments. What reason could there be to keep the Sabbath, observe dietary laws, practise circumcision, or even marry someone Jewish if the God of the Biblical and rabbinic tradition does not exist?

In an early response to such criticism, Rubenstein pointed out that the elimination of the religious framework of the Jewish faith does not undermine the sociological and psychological functions of Judaism. The ethic content of Judaism can persist even in the absence of religious faith. Judaism, he argued, is not simply a belief system - it is constituted of rituals and customs, which enable adherents of the tradition to celebrate life-cycle events and copy with crises. As Rubenstein explained:

> I do not believe that a theistic God is necessary for Jewish religious life...I have suggested that Judaism is the way in which we share the decisive times and crises of life through the traditions of our inherited community. The need for that sharing is not diminished in the time of the death of God.[10]

Yet despite this stance, Rubenstein believed it is nevertheless possible to view the cosmos as the expression of a single, unified and unifying source and ground which we name as God. If human beings are seen as an integral element of the cosmos, which is an expression of the Divine ground, then God is capable of thought, reflection and feeling.

Such a reversion to nature paganism parallels the return of the Jewish people to the land of Israel. Referring to traditional liturgy, Rubenstein pointed out that during the period of the diaspora Jews prayed that they be returned to the Holy Land. When this goal was attained, Jewish history had in principle come to an end, but since Rubenstein does not embrace polytheism, he argued that after Auschwitz and the return to Israel, the Divine manifested in nature was the God to whom Jews would turn in place of the God of history, especially in Israel. Rejecting the biblical view of a providential God, Rubenstein thus subscribed to a form of Canaanite nature paganism.

Over the years Rubenstein's earlier paganism lost its importance. He previously argued that when the Jewish people lived in their own country, they would revert to nature worship. But he eventually came to see that most Jews did not desire to live in Israel and those who settled there had no interest in nature paganism. Those who ceased to believe in God simply became secular Jews. But Rubenstein has parted company with these Jewish secularists; in mysticism he has found the God in whom he can believe after Auschwitz. 'I believe there is a conception of God', he writes, 'which remains meaningful after the death of the God-Who-acts-in-history. It is a very old conception of God with deep roots in both Western and Oriental mysticism. According to his conception, God is spoken of as the holy nothingness. When God is thus designated, He is conceived as the ground and source of all existence...God as the nothing is not absence of being but superfluity of being'. [11] Though such a view has affinities with other religions such as Buddhism, Rubenstein's position is far removed from the traditional understanding of God as the compassionate redeemer of Israel who lovingly watches over his chosen people.

Rubenstein's redefinition of God's nature avoids the dilemma of Divine theodicy, but it is meaningless for Jews who accept the traditional understanding of God. Rubenstein declares that after Auschwitz it is an illusion to believe in such a God and that each of us must accept that the universe is unconcerned with out lives, prayers and hopes. Yet it is just such a view that the theist rejects; what he seeks instead is a justification for God's ways, and that is what Rubenstein contends is impossible. To say that God is Divine nothingness merely confuses the issues. Thus rather than providing an adequate theodicy in the face of the horrors of the Holocaust, Rubenstein merely plunges the believer deeper into despair.

A Deistic Alternative

Unlike Wiesel and Rubenstein a number of Jewish thinkers have attempted to adopt a more positive theological stance. In the *Tremendum* published in 1981 Arthur A Cohen addressed the religious dilemmas raised by the Holocaust. Previously he had said nothing about the religious perplexities connected with the destruction of 6 million Jews in the Nazi era. In *The Natural and the Supernatural Jew* published in 1962 he had constructed a modern theology of Judaism without dealing with evil either in itself or in its horrific manifestation in the concentration camps. But in his later book Cohen uses the term 'tremendum' to designate an event of vast significance. Mindful of Rudolf Otto's characterisation of God's holiness as *mysterium tremendum*, Cohen argues that *mysterium tremendum* and *tremendum* convey the aspect of vastness and the resonance of terror. Yet these terms designate different realities. According to Cohen, the Holocaust was the human *tremendum*, the enormity of an infinitized man, who no longer seems to fear death, more to the point, fears it so completely, denies death so mightily, that the only patent of his refutation and denial is to build a mountain of corpses to the divinity of the dead'.[12] For Cohen the death camps were the *tremendum* since they represent an inversion of life to an orgiastic celebration of death. Like Otto's *mysterium tremendum*, Cohen's notion of the *tremendum* is meant to suggest a sense of unfathomable mystery. Cohen believes that the Holocaust was completely irrational and unique, and he doubts whether historians can understand its nature and significance.

Like Rubenstein, Cohen recognises that the Holocaust presented insurmountable difficulties for classical theism and for the Jewish understanding of God's relationship with the Jewish people. For Cohen post Holocaust theology must take account of three central elements: (1) God must abide in a universe in which God's presence and evil are both seen as real; (2) the relationship of God to all creation must be seen as meaningful and valuable; and (3) the reality of God is not isolated from God's involvement with creation. In formulating a theological response which embraces these features, he drew on Lurianic kabbalah as well as the philosophy of Franz Rosenzweig. According to Cohen, initially God was all in all and there was nothing else. But God overflowed absolute self-containment in a moment of love. For Cohen the world is God's created order, lovingly formed by the Divine word without the surrender of human freedom. Humanity is essential because without it the world would be unable to respond to God's love or personality.

Human beings, Cohen asserts have the capacity to respond to God since they partake of God's speech and freedom. According to Cohen, such freedom was intended to be tempered by reason, but this did not occur and therefore human freedom became the basis of the horrific events of the Holocaust. In advancing this view, Cohen criticises those who complain that God was silent during the events of the Holocaust. Such an assessment, Cohen notes, is a mistaken yearning for a non-existent interruptive God who is expected to interfere with earthly life. But if there were such a God, the created order would be an extension of the Divine realm, and there would be no opportunity for freedom. 'God is not the strategist of our particularities or our historical condition', he writes, 'but rather a mystery of futurity, always our posse, never our acts. If we can begin to see God less as the interferer whose insertion is welcome (when it accords with out needs) and more as the immensity whose reality is our prefiguration....we shall have won a sense of God whom we may love and honour, but whom we no longer fear and from whom we no longer demand'.[13]

Since Cohen does not believe that God acts in history, he dismisses the view that God was responsible for Auschwitz. Instead he asserts that God acts in the future. The Divine Life is 'a filament within the historical, but never the filament that we can identify and ignite according to our requirements'. Human beings, he believes, have the capacity to 'obscure, eclipse, burn out the Divine filament'.[14] God's role is not to act as a direct agent in human affairs, but as a teacher; His intention is to instruct human beings so as to limit their destructive impulses. For Cohen, Divine teaching is manifest in the halachah; in this way human freedom is granted within the framework of Jewish law. Given this conception of Divine action, God is in no way responsible for the horrors of the death camps - Auschwitz was the work of human beings who exercised their freedom for destruction and murder. According to Cohen such licence to act against God's will raises serious doubts about the viability of the State of Israel to protect the Jewish community from future disasters. The return to a homeland may prove more threatening even than genocide for, 'in no way is the Jew allowed any longer....to repeat his exile amid the nations, to disperse himself in order to survive'.[15] Further, Cohen asserts that dedication to the Holy Land devoid of a belief in a transcendent Deity can become a form of paganism. The founding of a Jewish state is thus not an adequate response to the religious perplexities posed by the Holocaust.

Although Cohen's redefinition of God's nature avoids the difficulties of seeing God as responsible for the events of the Holocaust, he has eliminated a fundamental aspect of Divine activity which is presupposed by Biblical and rabbinical Judaism. Throughout Jewish sources, God is understood as both transcendent and immanent - He created the universe and continuously sustains it. The God of the Jewish faith is the Lord of History. He guided His chosen people out of Egypt, revealed Himself on Mt.Sinai, delivered them up to the Promised Land, and providentially directs human history to its ultimate fulfilment in the world to come. Within this eschatological endeavour, God intervenes in history; He is a God who is present in everyday life. Conceiving God as a Divine filament in no sense corresponds with this traditional conception. Thus Cohen's solution to the problem of the Holocaust deprives the faith of a view of God which is central to the Jewish heritage. His response to the horrors of the death camps is unsatisfactory for those who seek an explanation how a benevolent God could have permitted the slaughter of 6 million innocent victims.

Traditional Jewish Theology

A number of theologians have been unwilling to alter the traditional understanding of God in attempting to make sense of the Holocaust. According to Eliezer Berkovits in *Faith after the Holocaust*, the modern Jewish response to the destruction of 6 million Jews should be modelled on Job's example. If there is no answer to the quest for an understanding of God's silence in the face of Nazi genocide, 'it is better to be without it than in the sham of....the humbug of a disbelief encouraged by people who have eaten their fill at the tables of a satiated society'.[16] At Auschwitz God was hidden, yet according to Berkovits in His hiddenness He was actually present. As hidden God, He is Saviour; in the apparent void He is the redeemer of Israel. How this is to be understood is shrouded in mystery. Berkovits writes that if Jewish faith is to be meaningful in the post-Holocaust age, the Jew must make room for the impenetrable darkness of the death camps within religious belief: 'The darkness will remain, but in its "light" he will make his affirmation. The inexplicable will not be explained, yet it will become a positive influence in the formulation of that which is to be acknowledged...perhaps in the awful misery of man will be revealed to us the awesome mystery of God.[17] The Holocaust is thus part of God's incomprehensible plan, defying rational justification and transcending human understanding.

Such argument is obviously not a solution to the problem of the Holocaust; rather it is a challenge to believe in God despite overwhelming obstacles. This evasion of the theological difficulties, while leaving room for blind faith, in no way explains how God could have allowed the Holocaust to take place. Berkovits claims that in His hiddenness, the hidden God is revealed and that He was both saviour and redeemer in the death camps. But how can this be so? For some Jews such an appeal to God's inscrutable plan merely aggravates and caricatures the horrors of the Nazi regime and deprives them of any firm foundation for religious belief. Thus Berkovits offers no help for those who are unable to follow Job's example, and instead seek a viable Jewish theodicy, in which the justice and righteousness of God are defended in the face of evil and suffering.

Another attempt to provide a Biblically based explanation for God's activity during the Nazi regime was proposed by Ignaz Maybaum in *The Face of God After Auschwitz*. In this study Maybaum argues that God has an enduring relationship with Israel, that He continues to act in history and that Israel has a divinely sanctioned mission to enlighten other nations. According to Maybaum the Holocaust is a result of God's intervention, but not as a Divine punishment. In explaining this view, he uses the crucifixion of Jesus as a model for understanding Jewish suffering during the Holocaust. Just as Jesus was an innocent victim whose death provides a means of salvation for humanity, so the deaths of the victims of the Holocaust were sacrificial offerings. Maybaum asserts that the Jews were murdered by the Nazis because they were chosen by God for this sacrifice. In this way God's purposes can be fulfilled. 'The Golgotha of modern mankind is Auschwitz', he asserts. 'The cross, the Roman gallows, was replaced by the gas chamber'.[18]

Maybaum contends that Jewish history was scarred by three major diasters which he designates by the Hebrew word *churban* - a term referring to an event of massive destructiveness. For Maybaum each *churban* was a divine intervention which had decisive significance for the course of history. The first of these cataclysmic occurrences was the destruction of Jerusalem in 586 B.C. which resulted in the diaspora of the Jewish community. This uprooting of the population was a catastrophe for the Nation, but it did inaugurate the Jewish mission to bring a knowledge of God and His laws to other peoples outside Israel's borders. In this respect the first *churban* was a manifestation of 'creative destructiveness'. The second *churban* was the Roman devastation of the second Temple in Jerusalem which inaugurated the establishment of the synagogue as the major focus of Jewish life where study and prayer replaced sacrifice. According to Maybaum, such activity is of a higher order than the sacrificial system of the Biblical period - this transformation of religious life was possible only through an act of destruction. Such an interpretation of the Jewish past runs counter to the traditional understanding of these events as divine punishment for the sinfulness of the nation.

The final *churban* was the Holocaust, an event in which the Jewish people were sacrificial victims in an event of creative destructiveness. In Maybaum's view God used the Holocaust to bring about the end of the Middle Ages, and usher in a new era of modernity. The sin for which the Jews died was the retention of remnants of the medieval European feudal structure. After the First World War the West could have transformed Eastern European society, but it did not act. As a result the devastation of the war served no purpose and Hitler was sent by God to bring about what the progressives failed to do. According to Maybaum, God used the Holocaust as a means to bring about the modern world. In this tragedy all that was medieval in character - including the majority of Eastern European Jews who lived in ghettos - had to perish. The murder of 6 million Jews was thus an act of creative destruction. With the elimination of the traditional Jewish community of Eastern Europe, world Jewry shifted to the United States, Western Europe, Russia and Israel. In these countries Jews were able to live in an emancipated environment which celebrated rationality and progress. Jews therefore suffer in order to bring about the rule of God over the world and its peoples; their God-appointed mission is to serve the course of historical progress and bring mankind into a new era. Only a part, though admittedly a traumatically large part of the Jewish people, was exterminated. The planned genocide of the Jewish people did not succeed, and Maybaum emphasises that the remnant that was saved had been selected by God as a perennial witness to His presence in the world and in the historical process. Of the sacrificial victims of Auschwitz he states categorically: 'Their death purged western civilisation so that it can again become a place where man can live, do justly, love mercy, and walk humbly with God'.[19]

Though this justification of the Holocaust is based on Biblical concepts, Maybaum's explanation will no doubt strike many as offensive. If God is benevolent, merciful and just in His dealings with mankind, how could He have intentionally planned the destruction of 6 million Jews? Surely through His omnipotence God could have brought about the redemption of the world without decimating His chosen people. Furthermore, the image of Hitler as God's instrument is a terrible and grotesque picture; to see God as a surgeon operating on the body of Israel, lacking pity for those who died in the process, is to make a mockery of God's eternal love. Unlike the ancient Israelites, whom God punished for their sins through the military intervention of Nebuchadnezzar, Jews who lost their lives in the camps were simply innocent victims of Nazi persecution. Thus Maybaum's conception of God as a slayer and saviour is hardly an adequate justification for God's apparent indifference to mass death, injustice, and suffering in the concentration camps.

Another traditional approach to the Holocaust is to see in the death camps a manifestation of God's will that His chosen people survive. Such a paradoxical view is most eloquently expressed by Emil Fackenheim in a series of publications in which he contends that God revealed Himself to Israel out of the furnaces of Auschwitz. For Fackenheim the Holocaust was the most disorienting event in Jewish history - a crisis which requires from the Jewish community a reassessment of God's presence in history. Through the Holocaust, he believes, God issued the 614th commandment: Jews are forbidden to grant posthumous victories to Hitler. According to Fackenheim, Jews are here instructed to survive as Jews. They are commanded to remember in their very guts and bowels the martyrs of the Holocaust, lest their memory perish: Jews are forbidden, furthermore, to deny or despair of God, however much they may have to contend with Him or with belief in Him. They are forbidden finally to despair of the world as the place which is to become the kingdom of God lest we help make it a meaningless place. 'We help make it a meaningless place in which God is dead or irrelevant and everything is permitted; to abandon any of these imperatives, in response to Hitler's victory at Auschwitz, would be to hand him yet other posthumous victories'.[20] For Fackenheim, it is a betrayal of the Jewish heritage to question whether the traditional Jewish conception of God can be sustained after the Holocaust.

In his later work, Fackenheim stresses that the Holocaust represents a catastrophic rupture with previously accepted views of Judaism, Christianity and western philosophy.[21] According to Fackenheim, the process of mending this rupture (*tikkun*) must take place in the scheme of life rather than of thought. The resistance to the destructive logic of the death camps constitutes the beginning of such repair. As Fackenheim explains: some camp inmates were unwilling to become 'muselmann' (those who were dead while still alive). Such resistance was exhibited by pregnant mothers who refused to abort their pregnancies hoping that their offspring would survive and frustrate the plans of the National Socialist Party to eliminate every Jew. Again other Jewish partisans took to the woods to fight the Nazis, and Hasidic Jews prayed even though they were forbidden to do so. Though the number of those who resisted the Nazis was small, they did exhibit that the logic of destruction could be overcome. These acts of resistance are of primary importance. it is not enough to understand the Holocaust - it must be resisted in flesh-and-blood action. In this connection, Fackenheim stresses that only as a consequence of the deed of resistance can resistive thought have any significance. The Holocaust was intended to give its victims no possibility of escaping the fate of becoming the living dead and subsequently dying in the gas chambers. The first act of resistance was the determination to survive or to die as a human being. The second step was to resist the nature of the logic of destruction. In the case of those victims who did resist, thought and action were interconnected: their recognition of the Nazi logic of destruction helped produce resistance to it - a life-and-death struggle that went on day and night.

Such resistance was more than self-protection. Since the Holocaust was a *novum* in history, this resistance was also a *novum*. As emphasised by Pelagia Lewinska, a Polish Roman Catholic, 'They had condemned us to die in our own filth', she wrote, 'to drown in mud, in our own excrement. They wished to abuse us, to destroy our human dignity. From the instant when I grasped the motivating principle...it was as if I had been awakened from a dream...I felt under orders to live and if I did die in Auschwitz, it would be as a human being, I would hold on to my dignity'.[22] Fackenheim views this statement as evidence of the ontological dimension of resistance and of a commanding voice. In the past when Jews were threatened, they bore witness to God through martyrdom but Fackenheim believes that such an act would have made no sense in the concentration camps. Such death was what the

Nazis hoped to accomplish. This resistance served as a new kind of sanctification; the refusal to die was a holy act. For Fackenheim those who heard God's command during the Holocaust were the inmates of camps who felt under an obligation to resist the logic of destruction. The rupture between the pre-Holocaust and post-Holocaust world must be mended by such resistance. Among the most significant Jewish acts of *tikkun* in the post-Holocaust world was the decision of the survivors of the Nazi period to make their homeland in Israel. Though Israel is continually endangered, the founding of a Jewish state represents a monumental attempt to overcome the Holocaust. For the first time in nearly two thousand years Jews have assumed responsibility for their own future. Furthermore, the establishment of a Jewish state is the precondition of post-Holocaust *tikkun* of Jewish-Christian relations. Before the Holocaust Jews depended on the majority for their welfare, but after the Holocaust Jews became the majority in their own country. In Israel the Jews became independent and produced weapons with which they could defend themselves. This transformation of Jewish life offers hope for the continuation of Jewish life after the tragic events of the Holocaust.

The difficulty with Fackenheim's view is that he does not attempt to justify his claim that Auschwitz was a revelation-event bearing Torah to twentieth-century Jews. This is simply asserted, yet it is not at all clear why this should be so. On the contrary, for many Jews the Holocaust has made it impossible to believe in the traditional Jewish picture of God as a Lord of history who has revealed His will to the Jewish people. For such Jews the world is a tragic and meaningless place where human beings have no basis for hope in Divine aid or in any ultimate solution of the ills that beset them. Though they might agree that the lesson of the Holocaust is that the Jewish people must survive against all odds, this would not be because of God's revelation in the death camps. Further, it is hard to see how Fackenheim's admonition to believe in God 'lest Judaism perish' could actually sustain religious belief. Trust in God is of a different order altogether from commitment to the Jewish people, and it is regrettable that Fackenheim fails to see the distinction.

Jewish Suffering and the Afterlife

These varied attempts to come to terms with the Holocaust all suffer from serious defects. As we have seen, Rubenstein rejects the traditional Jewish understanding of God's nature and activity and argues for a concept of Divine reality far-removed from the Jewish heritage. For Jewish traditionalists seeking to make sense of the horrors of the Holocaust such a suggestion offers no consolation or promise of hope. Cohen's conception of deism is also so remote from mainstream Jewish thought that it cannot resolve the religious perplexities posed by the death of 6 million Jews in the camps. Wiesel's agonizing struggle with religious doubt illuminates the theological problems connected with the events of the Nazi period but plunges the believer deeper into despair. At the other end of the spectrum the views of writers who have attempted to defend the Biblical and rabbinic concept of God are beset with difficulties. Maybaum's view that God used Hitler as an instrument for the redemption of mankind is a monstrous conception. Fackenheim's assertion that God issued the 614th commandment through the ashes of the death camps will no doubt strike many as wishful thinking. Finally Berhovits' view that God was hidden during the Nazi period offers no theological solution to the problem of suffering. These major Holocaust theologians have therefore not provided satisfactory answers to the dilemmas posed by the death camps. Contemporary Jewish theology is thus in a state of crisis both deepseated and acute: for the first time in history Jews seem unable to account for God's ways.

One element is missing from all these justifications of Jewish suffering; there is no appeal to the Hereafter. Though the Bible only contains faint references to the realm of the dead, the doctrine of Life after Death came into prominence during the Maccabean period when righteous individuals were dying for their faith. Subsequently the belief in the World to Come was regarded as one of the central tenets of the Jewish faith. According to rabbinic scholars, it was inconceivable that life would end at death: God's justice demanded that the righteous of Israel enter into a realm of eternal bliss where they would be compensated for their earthly travail. Because of this belief generations of Jews have been able to reconcile their belief in a benevolent and merciful God with the terrible tragedies they have endured. Through the centuries the conviction that the righteous would inherit eternal life has sustained generations of Jewish martyrs who suffered persecution and death. As Jews were slaughtered, they glorified God through dedication to the Jewish faith - such an act is referred to a *Kiddush ha-Shem* (Sanctification of the Divine Name). These heroic Jews who remained steadfast in their faith did not question the ways of God; rather their deaths testify to their firm belief in a providential Lord of history who would reserve a place for them in the Hereafter.

In Judaism this act of sanctification was a task for all Jews if the unfortunate circumstances arose. Thus through centuries of oppression *Kiddush ha-Shem* gave meaning to the struggle of Jewish warriors, strength of endurance under cruel torture, and a way out of slavery and conversion through suicide. In the Middle Ages repeated outbreaks of Christian persecution strengthened the Jewish determination to profess their faith, *Kiddush ha-Shem* became a common way of confronting missionary coercion - if Jews were not permitted to live openly as Jews, they were determined not to live at all. When confronted by force, Jews attempted to defend themselves, but chose death if this proved impossible. Thousands of Jews in the Middle Ages lost their lives. Some fell in battle, but the majority committed suicide for their faith. In the chronicles of this slaughter *Kiddush ha-Shem* was the dominant motif; Jews endeavoured to fight their assailants, but when their efforts failed they died as martyrs.

During the medieval period Jews also suffered because of the accusation that they performed ritual murders of Christian children, defamed Christianity in the Talmud, desecrated the Host, and brought about the Black Death. As they endured trials and massacres, they were fortified by the belief that God would redeem them in a future life. Repeatedly they proclaimed their faith in God and witnessed to the tradition of their ancestors. In later centuries *Kiddush ha-Shem* also became part of the history of Spanish Jewry. Under the fire and torture of the Inquisition chambers and tribunals Jews remained committed to their faith. the principles of *Kiddush ha-*

Shem supported multitudes of Jews as they faced calamity and death. The reality of their sacrifice and the image of their martyrdom became a dominant element in the Jewish consciousness. Due to the belief in divine reward, the Jewish community escaped disillusionment and despair in the face of tragedy: the courage of those who gave their lives to sanctify God's name became an inspiration to all those who faced similar circumstance. The history of the Jewish people thus bears eloquent testimony to the heroic martyrs who were convinced that reward in heaven would be vouchsafed to them if they remained faithful to God in their life on earth.

In the concentration camps as well many religious Jews remained loyal to the tradition of *Kiddush ha-Shem*. Joining the ranks of generations of martyrs, they sanctified God with unshakeable faith. As they awaited the final sentence, they drew strength from one another to witness to the God of Israel. In the camps many Jews faced death silently. When their last moments arrived they died without fear. They neither grovelled nor pleaded for mercy since they believed it was God's judgement to take their lives. With love and trust they awaited the death sentence. As they prepared to surrender themselves to God, they thought only of the purity of their souls. The martyrs of the concentration camps were convinced that their deaths would serve as a prelude to redemption. In Heaven they would receive their just reward, and by sanctifying God's name they could bring forgiveness to the Jewish people.

Conclusion

On the basis of the belief in eternal salvation which sustained the Jewish people through centuries of persecution, it might be expected that Holocaust theologians would attempt to explain the events of the Nazi period in the context of a future life. As we have seen, this has not occurred. Instead, these writers have set aside doctrines concerning messianic redemption, resurrection and final judgement. This shift in orientation is in part due to the fact that the views expressed in rabbinic literature are not binding. All Jews are obliged to accept the divine origin of the Law but this is not so with regard to theological concepts and theories expounded by the rabbis. Thus it is possible for a Jew to be religiously pious without accepting all the central beliefs of mainstream Judaism.

Given that there is no authoritative bedrock of Jewish theology, Holocaust theologians will no doubt have felt fully justified in ignoring various elements of traditional rabbinic eschatology which have ceased to retain their hold on Jewish consciousness. The doctrine of messianic redemption, for example, has been radically modified in contemporary Jewish thought. In this last century Reform Jews tended to interpret the new liberation in the Western world as the first step towards the realisation of the messianic dream: messianic redemption was understood in this-worldly terms. No longer, according to this view, was it necessary for Jews to pray for a restoration in Palestine; rather they should view their own countries as Zion and their political leaders as bringing about the messianic age. Secular Zionists, on the other hand, saw the return to Palestine as the legitimate conclusion to be drawn from the realities of Jewish life in Western countries, thereby viewing the state of Israel as a substitute for the messiah himself. Thus many modern Jews desire to view the messianic hope in naturalistic terms, abandoning the belief in a personal messiah.

Similarly, the doctrine of the resurrection of the dead has in modern times been largely replaced in both Orthodox and non-Orthodox Judaism by the belief in the immortality of the soul. The original belief in resurrection was an eschatological hope bound up with the rebirth of the nation in the days of the messiah. But as this messianic concept faded into the background so did this doctrine. For most Jews physical resurrection is simply inconceivable in the light of a scientific understanding of the nature of the world. The late British chief rabbi, J.H.Hertz, for example, argued that what really matters is the doctrine of the immortality of the soul. Thus he wrote: 'Many and various are the folk beliefs and poetical fancies in the rabbinical writings concerning Heaven and Hell. Our most authoritative religious guides, however, proclaim that no eye hath seen, nor can mortal fathom, what awaiteth us in the Hereafter; but that even the tarnished soul will not forever be denied spiritual bliss'.

In the Reform community a similar attitude prevails. In a well-known statement of beliefs of Reform Judaism it is stated that Reform Jews 'reassert the doctrine of Judaism that the soul is immortal, grounding his belief on the Divine nature of the human spirit, which forever finds bliss in righteousness and misery in wickedness. We reject as ideas not rooted in Judaism the belief in bodily resurrection in Hell and Paradise as abodes for eternal punishment or reward'. The point to note about the conception of the immortal soul in both Orthodox and Reform Judaism is that it is disassociated from traditional notions of messianic redemption and divine judgement. The belief in eternal punishment has also been discarded by a large number of Jews partly because of the interest in penal reform during the past century. Punishment as retaliation in a vindictive sense has been generally rejected. The value of punishment as a deterrent or in the protection of society is widely accepted. But the emphasis today is on the reformatory aspects of punishment. In the light of this shift in emphasis the question of reward and punishment in a theological sense is approached in a questioning spirit. Further, the rabbinic view of Hell is seen by many as morally repugnant. Jewish theologians have stressed that it is a delusion to believe that a God of love could have created a place of eternal punishment.

Due to this shift in emphasis in Jewish thought, it is not surprising that Jewish Holocaust theologians have refrained from appealing to the traditional belief in other-worldly reward and punishment in formulating their responses to the horrors of the death camps. Yet without this belief, it is simply impossible to make sense of the world as the creation of an all-good and all-powerful God. Without the eventual vindication of the righteous in Paradise, there is no way to sustain the belief in a providential God who watches over His chosen people. The essence of the Jewish understanding of God is that he loves His chosen people. If death means extinction, there is no way to make sense of the claim that He loves and cherishes all those who died in the concentration camps - suffering and death would ultimately triumph over each of those who perished. But if there is eternal life in a World to Come, then there is hope that the righteous will share in a divine life. Moreover, the divine attribute of justice demands that the righteous of Israel who met their death as innocent victims of the Nazis will reap an everlasting reward. Here then is an answer to the religious perplexities of the Holocaust. The promise of immortality offers a way of reconciling the belief in a loving and just God with the nightmare of the death camps. As we have seen, this hope sustained the Jewish people through centuries of suffering and martyrdom. Now that Jewry stands on the threshold of the twenty-first century, it must again serve as the fulcrum of religious belief. Only this way will the Jewish people who have experienced the Valley of the Shadow of Death be able to say in the ancient words of the Psalmist: 'I shall fear no evil for thou art with me'.

NOTES

1. E.Wiesel, *Nights* (Bantam Books, 1982). As quoted by R. Rubenstein and J. Roth *Approaches to Auschwitz* (SCM Press,1987), p.283.

2. Ibid., p.285.

3. E.Wiesel, *The Trial of God* (Random House, 1979) p.129.

4. Ibid., p.133.

5. R. Rubenstein and J. Roth, op.cit., p.287.

6. E.Wiesel, *A Jew Today* (Random House, 1978) p.136.

7. Ibid., p.164.

8. R. Rubenstein, *After Auschwitz* (Bobbs Merrill, 1966), p.153.

9. R. Rubenstein and J. Roth, *Approaches to Auschwitz* (SCM Press, 1987).

10. R. Rubenstein *After Auschwitz* as quoted by R. Rubenstein and J. Roth *op cit.* pp.312-13.

11. *Ibid.*,p.315.

12. A. Cohen, *Tremendum* (Crossroad Publishing Company, 1981) as quoted by R. Rubinstein and J. Roth, *op.cit.* p.330).

13. *Ibid.*, p.331.

14. *Ibid.*, p.332.

15. *Ibid.*, p.333.

16. E. Berkovits, *Faith after the Holocaust* (Ktav Publishing House Inc., 1973) pp. 5-6.

17. *Ibid.*, p.70.

18. I. Maybaum, *The Face of God After Auschwitz* (Polak and Van Gennep, 1965) p.36.

19. *Ibid.*, p.84.

20. E. Fackenheim, *Judaism* XVI 1967) 272-3.

21. E. Fackenheim, *To Mend the World* (Schoken Books, 1982).

22. *Ibid.*, p.250.

JEWISH STUDIES

1. S. Daniel Breslauer, Meir Kahane: Ideologue, Hero, Thinker
2. David B. Griffiths, A Critical Bibliography of Writings on Judaism (2 vols.)
3. Allen Howard Podet, The Success and Failure of the Anglo-American Committee of Inquiry, 1945-1946: Last Chance in Palestine
4. Leonard S. Kravitz, The Hidden Doctrine of Maimonides' *Guide for the Perplexed*: Philosophical and Religious God-Language in Tension
5. Martin Lockshin (trans.), Rabbi Samuel Ben Meir's Commentary on Genesis: An Annotated Translation
6. Philip Desind, Jewish and Russian Revolutionaries Exiled To Siberia, 1901-1917
7. Rachel Feldhay Brenner, A. M. Klein, The Father of Canadian Jewish Literature: Essays in the Poetics of Humanistic Politics
8. Shimon Shokek, Jewish Ethics and Jewish Mysticism in *Sefer Ha-Yashar* (Roslyn Weiss, Hebrew trans.)
9. Mareleyn Schneider, History of a Jewish Burial Society: An Examination of Secularization
10. S. Daniel Breslauer, The Hebrew Poetry of Hayyim Nahman Bialik (1873-1934) and a Modern Jewish Theology
11. Bat-Ami Zucker, U.S. Aid to Israel and Its Reflection in *The New York Times* and *The Washington Post* 1948-1973: The Pen, The Sword, and The Middle East
12. David S. Williams, Stylometric Authorship Studies in Flavius Josephus and Related Literature
13. Lawrence J. Epstein, The Theory and Practice of Welcoming Converts to Judaism: Jewish Universalism
14. Yakov Rabkin and Ira Robinson (eds.), The Interaction of Scientific and Jewish Cultures in Modern Times
15. Shimon Shokek, Repentance in Jewish Ethics, Philosophy and Mysticism
16. Dan Cohn-Sherbok (editor), Divine Interventions and Miracles in Jewish Theology
17. William E. Kaufman, The Evolving God in Jewish Process Theology
18. Dan Cohn-Sherbok (editor), Theodicy